CHILDREN'S LIBRARIAN, STALKER, CORPSE

Susan Ei, the FBI, and Pequot Library, Southport, Connecticut

by Henry Berry

© 2024 Henry Berry

Henry Berry is the author of:

A Clicking in the Air — A Connecticut Whistleblower's Story
Massacre in Newtown — Adam Lanza's Dark Passage to Madness
Let There Be Links — The Sources and Nature of Internet Religion
The Refuge of Surfaces — A Poetics of Surfaces and the Postmodern Odyssey
A Passion for Innocence — Sex and Sexuality in the Paintings of John Currin

CHAPTERS

INTRODUCTION – FBI Infiltration of the Pequot Library, Southport, Connecticut

Susan Ei was children's librarian from 2005 to 2017 at the Pequot Library in Southport, Connecticut. Southport is an enclave of Fairfield known for its exceptional wealth. While Pequot library is an association library supported mostly by donations from individuals and businesses and other organizations and is distinct from Fairfield's main public library and the one branch, Pequot Library is nonetheless considered a part of the town library system. About a third of Pequot Library's annual operating funds come from the town of Fairfield.

Having grown up in Fairfield, I always knew about Pequot Library. But it wasn't until the mid 1980s that I started going to the library regularly two or three times a week. I had rented a post office box at the Southport post office to have a permanent business address as I was moving around to different apartments or shared houses every couple of years. I was a small, entrepreneurial businessperson pursuing various activities. Among these were freelance writing, tutoring, teaching creative writing at adult education programs, and book reviewing.

The Pequot Library was only about a quarter mile west of the Southport post office. So I would make a stop at it when I was in Southport checking my mail. I soon found that the library was congenial to my interests in literature, history, biography, and art, and also to my preference for a smaller, quiet, pleasant location where I could read, do research, and work without distractions. Pequot Library was popular and well supported by the surrounding community, but it was rarely bustling. It held exhibitions, and offered programs for children and adults. But there were no large numbers of persons at the library for exhibitions or programs during the midday hours when I was usually there.

With an M.A in philosophy from Georgetown University following a B.A. in philosophy from Fairfield University, I found the sorts of books Pequot purchased as new books for its collection in the areas of history, literature, biography, and art especially appealing. I also liked it that Pequot had a national reputation for its collection of Americana. American history and biographies were of particular interest to me as was Connecticut and New England history as a lifelong resident of the state which was one of the original colonies.

Susan Ei found the Pequot Library congenial for the same reasons as well. She began working there in the early 2000s doing varied tasks such as working at the circulation desk, checking in new arrivals, answering the phone, and returning books to stacks. In 2005, she was given the position of children's librarian when the woman holding the position left it to go west when her husband was transferred to a new job.

With her education, competence, initiative, and personableness, Susan was the right person for the position. Pequot Library did not have to look far for an ideal replacement for children's librarian. Susan moved into the position smoothly, as if she had held it for years. Before long she was devising innovative educational and activity programs for children, brought a unique vibrancy to the children's reading sessions, and created an environment that was distinctive, welcoming, and stimulating. Susan and her children's section of the Pequot Library became another one of the widely recognized and appreciated aspects of the library.

Susan had no inkling of the sorrows and pressures that lay ahead of her in the years to come when she took over as children's librarian of Pequot Library with her characteristic enthusiasm and optimism.

I date the FBI's targeting of me for particular and particularly vile targeting in 2012 or thereabouts. I don't remember the exact date because by that time in my ongoing exposure of crime and corruption throughout the Connecticut legal system, I was being targeted by different elements of law enforcement and individuals in the legal field and their accomplices. I was trying to take the targeting in stride, even though with death threats and regular instances of menacing, I knew that harm could befall me any day. I tried to live my life as normally as possible while being continuously wary and defensive. I didn't take the time to record every incident or try to expose the deeper layers of what I was experiencing and recognizing.

It was at the Fairfield Public Library about this time that the FBI signaled it was targeting me in particular. As I was walking through the expensive main area of the library, to my left a man I walked toward made motions with his upper body and his arms and hands so that I could not help but notice him. He was holding the spine of a book out toward me, motioning it back and forth at me. I could see on the spine in large letters the word "Taliban." The FBI was signaling me that for my investigative journalism activity exposing crime and corruption throughout the Connecticut legal system, I was being seen as an enemy of the state.

After this experience at the Fairfield Public Library, I begin integrating my experiences and knowledge of the FBI into my investigative journalism. The FBI animus against me for exposing crime and corruption among individuals and organizations they had affinities with in Connecticut now unfolded into new ways and new dimensions in targeting me.

Knowing from its surveillance of me that I made regular stops at the Pequot Library, like stores and other libraries I frequented, it became a locus for FBI defamation and activities to let me know that I was despised. My presence at and relations with staff of the Pequot library became special targets of the FBI from seeing from its surveillance that I had cordial relations and sometimes friendly chats with staff members and even at times seeing incidents where I was helpful to staff or patrons such as when I was would consult with someone on some book they had questions about or one time was asked by a custodian to help move a harpsichord in the library auditorium that was going to be used in a musical performance.

The FBI hostility toward me at the Pequot Library culminated in an August 25, 2015, targeting incident of me when I was working on my computer at a table in the main reading room which I felt was threatening, as it was intended to be, and saw as a step toward greater, unknown future such incidents. In this incident, a woman undoubtedly connected to the FBI came close to me slightly behind my left shoulder and thrust a camera toward my head a few times in a menacing way while clicking it to convey to me that she was taking photographs of me, as one for example sees in films that a spy or assassin would take photographs of someone they were targeting. As I recollected on this incident after having experienced it, I recognized that at least two library staff members had participated with the woman with the camera in lulling me into thinking that everything was normal at the library that day as FBI people including two or three others besides the woman with the camera in effect surrounded me to spring the unnerving incident when I would least expect it and was most vulnerable.

It was after I was barred from the library under threat of arrest for trespass for having brought the incident up to the executive director and then filed a lawsuit against the library and certain individuals connected to it when the FBI enlisted Susan Ei into becoming part of its harassment and threatening program of me. With Susan's upper-level position at the library and using her in its targeting program distances from the library, Susan became a primary instrument in the

FBI's signaling to me that its targeting program knew no bounds and that the means and forms it took were unpredictable for me, and I was defenseless against them.

With Susan Ei put to the harassment of me, the FBI signaled new levels of danger to me and disruptions of my life, as I expected from the number of individuals and the effort of organization and timing of the August 25, 2015, incident at the Pequot Library. Susan Ei did not know what was really going on, and did not realize the danger the FBI had put her in.

1. Familiar Faces

I never actually met Susan Ei, not in a formal way where we were introduced to each other or exchanged names. I don't remember the first time I saw her either. But it must have been one day in the early 2000s when she appeared behind the circulation desk by the main reading room of the Pequot Library in Southport, Connecticut, a new member of library staff.

By then I had been a patron of the Pequot Library for over 20 years. I began going to the library regularly two or three times a week for an hour or two at a time as a change of scenery from working at home on various self-employment businesses over the years including desk-top publisher, author and publisher consultant, book marketer, and free-lance writer. Pequot Library also drew me because of its local reputation as a library with an important collection of Americana books, prints, and documents, its literary and art exhibitions, its acquisitions of new books in the areas of history and art displayed in the main reading room, and its small size and quiet atmosphere.

Pequot Library was also known throughout New England, along the Eastern seaboard states, and into the Midwest for its annual book sale. This sale drew book dealers and collectors from as far away as Florida. In the annual book sale's heyday from the 1980s to early 2000s, in the day's leading up to the sale, vans and campers with license plates from such states as Maine, Pennsylvania, Ohio, and Virginia would park along the side streets by the library so their owners could obtain the prized lower-number admission slips given out the Thursday before the sale's 9:00AM opening on Friday so they could be among the first in the inevitable rush to look among the tens of thousands of books for sale to find the most desirable ones. For many years, as book dealer myself among my varied occupations, I was one of those showing up on the Thursday hours before the late afternoon time when the numbered admission slips would be given out to get one of the lower numbers.

Since the Pequot Library is small and its staff is not large, Susan and I would naturally notice each other; and as usual between regular patrons and staff, say hello or nod to each other in passing. Rarely checking out books at Pequot Library and familiar with library organization and how to research from my work and interests, I did not interact with her, nor any other Pequot employee, in checking out or returning books or asking directions about how to find what I was looking for. Nonetheless, we soon recognized each other as being associated with Pequot Library and familiar faces at it.

My first memory of Susan Ei as an individual outside of her routine tasks as an employee at the circulation desk and interactions with patrons checking out or returning books was one day when she had a bandage wrapped around the palm of one her hands extending to her wrist as well. I noticed the bandage when seeing her that day behind the circulation desk, but didn't ask about it. Not long after while I was working at one of the desks in the main room, Susan came out from behind the desk to do something, perhaps put a newspaper someone had been reading back on the shelf where daily papers were placed. The reading room is not large, and I could not help seeing her moving about in it. Besides me and now Susan, there was another man who was standing in the room. As Susan passed near him to return to the circulation desk, seeing the bandage, the man asked, "What happened to your hand?"

"I burned it grabbing a hot pot," Susan answered.

The man had a word of sympathy. But that was it. Susan paused a moment out of politeness, then continued her way to back behind the circulation desk.

The reason I remember this incident is not only because it was my first glimpse of Susan outside of her role as circulation employee, but also because of the simplicity and directness of the brief words between Susan and the man. I saw that Susan was a no-drama individual, and her straightforwardness, simplicity, and manner were foundational and fetching. There was a freshness and openness to her, the freshness of openness, and she was easy to engage with and readily engaged with others.

Her humaneness was evident as well. She offered no excuse for her absentminded mistake in grabbing the hot pan causing a temporary injury requiring a bandage presumably over a salve. Nor did she look for sympathy. No "how dumb of me" from Susan angling for a listener such as the man to bolster her by a reply such as "we all do something like that occasionally." Susan knew she had done something dumb. It was evident. She knew as well that such kinds of mistakes were not unusual.

Neither was there any note of remorse in Susan's voice. She didn't regret her mistake because she knew that she was intelligent and experienced enough not to have done it in the first place. She had made a mistake, and what happened was natural. No denying, blaming, or obscuring the natural for Susan. It was almost as if her simplicity of nature banished a sense of fate; although I'm sure she was aware that there were matters and events outside of her control finding their way into her life. Susan's honesty would not allow a blindness to fate. Yet as she knew, she was an individual, and this made her responsible.

Knowing she was the agent of her own destiny, of her own life, Susan was not given to intrigue or conspiracy, means malevolent others use to destroy agency in the lives of others and devise a destiny of their own making for those they target. Susan's ambition and effect was to engender in others an appreciation for independence, to implant or enhance awareness of their own best potentials and guidance in how to reach these, and to nurture a community where education, play, respect, friendship, and growth were provided.

I don't remember just when Susan became children's librarian of the Pequot Library. I learned by being at the Pequot Library off and on and simply seeing and hearing what was going on, not by anyone telling me, that the woman who had been the children's librarian had moved to the West coast with her husband, and Susan was no longer behind the circulation desk where I usually saw her, but at the desk in the children's area of the library. Not knowing anything in particular about Susan such as her education, interests, desires, I presumed that this was a variation, not a change, of her position at the library — circulation clerk directed to sit at the desk of the children's area so it would not look forlorn or overlooked as children and their mothers or nannies came in during the day. Some library employee would have to be a presence to give life to the children's area and help patrons young and old. I assumed that this was Susan's job now when she was in according to her normal schedule. If not Susan, then another employee when she would have been in during her normal work schedule. I presumed this arrangement was temporary until the library found another full-time children's librarian.

I learned Susan had been appointed full-time Pequot Library children's librarian as I was standing near the circulation desk one day looking at some flyers placed on a table near it. Susan came to the desk from the direction of the children's area to get something, maybe scissors or paper clips. Susan took her time with whatever brought her to the desk, lingering.

The woman at the circulation desk for that day knew what was going on. "How's it going," the woman asked. "Nervous?" But she knew the answer.

Susan looked at the woman, and nodded, She seemed drawn into herself, concentrated. She wasn't though shrinking from something, rather formulating something and preparing for it.

I found before long from one of the flyers Susan had scheduled a children's event coming up in a couple of weeks. Susan was naturally anxious, and in this case, modestly and openly as was her way, reaching out for support from other library employees. Though capable as she knew and as evident to others in that she had been selected to be the children's librarian, this was not a position she had ever held. It was new to her.

Susan's first children's event was a success. It was the first of many to come in the years she was children's librarian which would make the children's library a destination for children, parents, and teachers.

Susan and I never came to know each other much. Since the Pequot Library is small, its space for patrons all on one floor, we couldn't help seeing each other two or three times when we were there at the same time. I would often see her when I used the copy machine which was near the children's area, or when I was looking at art exhibitions on a wall near the children's area. Or I'd see Susan when she would sometimes come out to the circulation desk just off the main reading room to get something or have a word with the staff member there. And she'd see me working at one of the desks.

Often when I was working at one of the desks, I'd have a stack of books I had bought at an estate sale earlier in the day or brought in from my inventory in my apartment beside my computer to research for descriptions to include in my online listings of them and to find current prices for them. From working at the circulation desk at first and then from seeing me in the library after being appointed children's librarian, Susan recognized I was involved in the field of antiquarian books in some way. Seeing me at the annual Pequot Library book sales and occasionally purchase a book from the books-for-sale bookcase the Library had near the circulation desk went along with this limited knowledge Susan and other staff had of me. Sometimes staff members would ask me something about an old book they had always had around at home or had bought at some tag sale.

Susan and I rarely spoke directly to each other. The few times in over the decade she had been at the library I spoke to her were when I asked if the children's area was going to be empty for a half an hour or so when I was looking for a place to do some work when there was no room in the main reading room or the two small rooms off it. I wanted to make sure there was no children's event planned or would not interfere with anything Susan would be doing.

One time when I was looking at books displayed in one of the glass cases in the hallway connecting the children's area and the main part of the library, Susan stopped to see what I was looking at. We had a word on the antiquarian book on display. I don't remember how the brief conversation went, but I do remember Susan mentioned the term "front free end page." This is the first page in a book, and it is usually blank. In the case of the book we were both perusing in the display case, the front free end page may have been what was being highlighted because of an author signature, bookplate, or some other point of special interest about the book.

Though unexpected, Susan's use of the term didn't surprise me since she obviously had an interest in books in being associated with the library. However, with her using this term, I saw her interest in books went beyond the usual even by library employee standards. There's not many who, library employee or anyone else, would use the term in relation to the part of the book Susan and I were looking at. The term is rarely used in conversation. It is familiar mostly from book descriptions in library or auction catalogues with details of books of interest to persons with advanced interest in books. For instance, note of a "front free end page" could indicate if a book had been rebound or not, a point which could affect a book's history or price. Often "front free end page" is abbreviated "FFEP." As long as I have been interested in books, eventually becoming a bookseller, I did not learn the term for many years; though when I did, it's meaning was immediately clear to me from having by then seen tens of thousands of front free end pages and having come to understand why it may at times be noted in book cataloging and book selling.

2. The FBI's Pathway to the Pequot Library

Sometime in or about 2012, in a strange incident at the Fairfield Public Library, I was informed that I was being seen as equivalent to Taliban undoubtedly for my recounting of my experiences of widespread, chronic crime and corruption throughout the Connecticut legal system. Much of this has been narrated in my book "A Clicking in the Air — A Connecticut Whistleblower's Story" covering experiences of mine and related perceptions and deductions in the decade of the 2000s before the incident at the Fairfield Public Library. I describe this book as a first-person true-crime narrative in the manner of creative nonfiction.

The last sentence of "A Clicking in the Air" is "That is another story." The other story is the FBI targeting of me since 2012 or thereabouts. "A Clicking in the Air" is about crime and corruption I encountered in the Connecticut state legal system. The story revolves around Pullman and Comley law firm lawyers James T. Shearin and Timothy A. Bishop stealing close to $6,000 in medical films meant for an operation on my neck. They were representing me as plaintiff in a car accident causing nerve damage in my neck requiring surgery to alleviate. Apparently I was not a welcome client for them, and they sabotaged my case and ruined any chance I had of obtaining a relevant settlement. With respect to the lawyer Shearin, I see in retrospect that my experience with him and the Pullman and Comley law firm began with a lie and ended with a theft. The lie, told to me in my first conversation on the phone with Shearin, was that the husband of the woman who crashed into me causing my injuries, a well-to-do accountant with a home in Trumbull and office in Fairfield, was not a client of the law firm. It was about two years after I finally had the operation on my neck when I was pursuing a civil case against Shearin, Bishop, and the Pullman and Comley law firm that I learned that the accountant had been a client. With respect to the lawyer Bishop, he was ignorant of elementary anatomy and he misled me about options available to me for having and paying for the surgery and resources of the defendant and her accountant husband that would have covered the cost of the surgery and also a relevant settlement. (Later Shearin became chairman of the law firm. Bishop left Pullman and Comley not long after I moved to another lawyer.)

The Pullman and Comley lawyers Shearin and Bishop denied I had ever left medical films with them. "Berry is lying" is what they told to other members of the law firm and anyone else who asked. They implied I was engaging in extortion and defamation. I was an example of the proverbial "disgruntled client," so they maintained.

In the course of one of my lawsuits, quite unexpectedly, serendipitously, in going through documents in the office of the lawyer I had moved to out of confusion and desperation over what was going on with my personal-injury case, I turned up Pullman and Comley office records confirming that I had dropped off my medical films. In the law firm's lengthy, detailed office record of activity in my case, in an entry at a date about the time I had said I had dropped off the films was a listing of my medical films costing some $5800.00. One reason the record was kept was for costs in the case I would be reimbursed for in the event I won the case.

Before I found the Pullman and Comley office record listing my medical films meant for a neck operation for nerve damage, I had filed a complaint against the Pullman and Comley lawyers James T. Shearin and Timothy A. Bishop for mishandling of property of mine left with them at their request and multiple violations of legal ethics and professional standards with the Statewide Grievance Committee supposedly overseeing lawyer ethics and practices in the state of Connecticut. In Shearin and Bishop's reply to my grievance complaint, they denied I had dropped off my medical films with them. The Grievance Committee dismissed my complaint.

After turning up undeniable evidence that I had dropped off my medical films at the Bridgeport office of the Pullman and Comley law firm — office records recording that the films had been dropped off — I presented this evidence to the Statewide Grievance Committee requesting a reversal of the ruling of dismissal of my complaint on the ground that Shearin and Bishop had undoubtedly, demonstrably, lied to the Committee about having received my medical films. In this case, the Committee ruled that the theft was "immaterial," thus upholding the ruling of dismissal and ratifying the lie of Shearin and Bishop which was not only a lie to me and criminal cover up of a theft, but also a lie to the Grievance Committee. There you are about lawyer ethics.

After this, I filed a criminal complaint with the Bridgeport police. I had first reported the theft to the Fairfield County state's attorney's office at the Bridgeport Superior Court on Main Street, and been told that the complaint should be filed there. In making the complaint at the Bridgeport police department, I mentioned that I had been at the state's attorney's office, and been told that the Bridgeport police department was the appropriate place to file such a complaint. The Bridgeport police then handed my complaint over to the state's attorney's office since I had been there first, and no one wanted it to appear that I was "forum shopping", i. e., shopping my complaint around to find a law-enforcement agency that would handle it favorably.

Getting the complaint from the Bridgeport police department, state's attorneys quickly illegally obtained a warrant to tap my phone. I proved this by later getting a default judgment in a civil case upon the defendants (state's attorneys and the office of state's attorney) refusing to turn over to me for inspection the application for a wiretap on my phone, which application would surely contain false statements made to judges who would make a decision on the application. Like the Pullman and Comley lawyers Shearin and Bishop, state's attorneys were now saying I was a criminal. The illegal wiretap was accompanied by serial attempts to entrap me for some drug and/or sex charge. This is one episode of "A Clicking in the Air."

I found the implication that I was comparable to Taliban for pursuing legal options and procedures in trying to deal with what had turned into multiple, manifold crimes and wrongful acts against me by multiple individuals at different organizations in the private and public sectors to be so outrageous that I began posting reports and comments on this and related matters such as the theft and the crime and corruption I encountered in the legal system. Despite knowing that there was no doubt that I had been the victim of theft by lawyers Shearin and Bishop of the Pullman and Comley law firm and I had proven that Connecticut state's attorneys had illegally wiretapped my phone, the FBI targeted me, bizarrely identifying me as Taliban.

In response to my postings of reports and comments now including FBI targeting of me, the FBI, not surprisingly, escalated and elaborated its targeting of me to include a numerous and changing cast of agents, defamation and demonization of me to store clerks and managers, disruption of my activities in the antiques field, and interference with my personal and business relationships. My main interest in the antiques field is ephemera of special interest in all areas of culture — historical, scientific, artistic, literary, legal, etc. I purchase, research, catalog, and market diverse material in these areas for sale to specialized dealers and research libraries and private and public institutions, listing at online sales sites such as eBay, and consignment to auctions. Libraries are obviously a prime resource for me. I'm on the computer for research, word-processing item descriptions, uploads of items for sale, email interaction with prospective buyers, making up mailing labels, etc., for six hours or more nearly every day.

I get out to libraries whenever I can to do some of this work as a change of scenery from my home office. Pequot Library in Southport, Connecticut, was one of the area libraries I went to regularly, usually in conjunction with checking mail at my post office box at the Southport U. S. post office, a business address I have had for decades. The Fairfield Public Library and Fairfield University DiMenna-Nyselius Library were other area libraries I went to regularly. The librarians at these libraries recognized me as a familiar face, and I had conversations with some of them about research I was doing and in some cases, about their personal lives. For instance, I knew that the daughter of one librarian was graduating from Wellesley College in Massachusetts, and that another one and her husband had had a child and were moving to a different town mainly for the exceptional day-care services it offered for residents.

The FBI targeting involving harassment, overt menacing, and defamation of me to induce others to participate in the FBI's denigration and marginalization of me occurred in all the libraries I went to. However, in time, it became concentrated at the Pequot Library. The way I see this is that with the Pequot Library's small staff and small space, the FBI saw it as the best library to engage in its most nefarious plans with the likelihood of not being exposed. Fewer individuals would have to be involved in any provocative, threatening targeting — thus low chance of having someone alert me or making the FBI's scheme at the library public. And with small space, greater likelihood provocative, threatening targeting would not be observed by anyone not involved in it. In short, the Pequot Library offered the FBI greater control over its nefarious plans.

Although I could not be aware of the FBI's ultimate aim, FBI involvement with Pequot Library staff was not unrecognized by me. First signs were men who volunteered to work on the annual book sale coming into the main reading room when I was there sitting in a chair reading or at a table working at my computer. It was obvious someone with the FBI had pointed me out, and pointed me out as someone to be harassed.

Such men had never appeared in the main reading room in the decades I had been going to the Library. Nearly all the time they were at the Library volunteering, they were in the basement where books for the sale were stored as they were brought in from the shed near the entrance to the Library parking lot where patrons and others dropped them off. The volunteers would sort the books, price them, and store them in boxes piled one upon another ready to be moved out of the basement to tables set up in different parts of the library and surrounding outside areas as the days of the annual summer sale approached. Most of the men were older, retired. Volunteering was something useful for them to do, and they enjoyed the camaraderie of their shared time in the basement.

The first incident signaling to me that my presence at the Pequot Library had been brought to the attention of individuals connected with the library occurred sometimes during the presidential campaign of 2015 when one of the men, elderly, tall, and thin, came into the main reading room as I was sitting in a low, roomy chair near the fireplace. I could not help but see him stride into the room from the direction of the circulation desk because the chair was facing that way. His rapid movement and darting eyes indicated he was not looking for anything such as a newspaper or intending to take a chair. I remember he seemed to tower over me in the low chair as he stopped to my left at about a forty-five degree angle where I could not help but see he had done so. He and I were the only ones in the room, and his rapid appearance with rapid, somewhat jerky movements attracted my notice.

As I looked toward him vaguely wondering what was going on with him, taking half a step toward me and looking directly at me, he uttered in a tone of contempt, "You going to be voting? Did you watch…?". I don't recall what the man asked me if I had watched — some political event involving a presumed presidential candidate recently in the news which I was aware of, but hadn't paid much attention to beyond glancing at media reports on it. This was in the late spring of 2015 when the presidential campaigns of contenders for a party's nomination for president were beginning to heat up before their party's nomination at the conventions in 2016. The man spoke as if he were demanding that I pay close attention to the event even though it had passed.

"No, I didn't," I replied. "I don't pay much attention to what's going on this early. I wait until a nominee is selected, and then start paying more attention."

Satisfied that he had exposed me for the unpatriotic ignoramus that the FBI had told him I was and that he had performed his public duty as a concerned citizen as the FBI advised him he ought to, the witless fool left the room. I went back to my reading. The incident exemplifies the inane posturing and pointlessness of the FBI targeting, not that it is not menacing and threatening. The FBI means to actually menace and threaten individuals and in most cases, including mine, cause actual psychological and as possible when the FBI thinks it can get away with it, physical injury or death. The contrived, expedient display of "values" supposedly being threatened by such as me inherent in the FBI targeting incidents whether by agents or accomplices reveals not only the mindlessness and silliness of FBI activity, but also its nihilism and poverty. Such stunts, such performances lay bare the clown-like mentality, the FBI's fears about its legitimacy, and its hostile posture toward normality to ones attuned to pick up on this. As I've realized in the years of being targeted, the most informative study for gaining an understanding of the FBI is abnormal, deviant psychology.

The next incident involved both a book-sale volunteer and a Pequot staff member. The staff member's name was Cheryl. She had blond hair, a somewhat roundish nose. I wish I could remember her full name to tell you, but I can't.

The book-sale volunteer, like the previous one believing he was belittling me as I sat in the chair indifferent to him, came out from the basement and took a place in the main reading room as I sat at one of the tables looking through a newly acquired art book I had taken from a shelf where it was displayed. This volunteer, shorter and heavy-set, took a chair behind me, off my right shoulder. I had to turn most of the way around to see him. Cheryl in coordination as evident for her role in the simple scheme, moved out from behind the circulation desk to take a place in my line of sight, where I could see her by raising my head straight up from looking through the art book.

Seeing Cheryl out of the top of my eyes stationing herself where I could not help but notice her and aware of the book-sale volunteer who had stationed himself behind me off to my right, I wondered what now I was going to face in the targeting which I was seeing was becoming more extensive by involving more individuals at the library and also becoming systematic in that it would be continual.

I looked over at Cheryl. Though obviously stationing herself where I could not help see her, she did not look back at me even to acknowledge my presence as a longtime patron of the library she had seen countless times. She faced mostly toward me, but her upper body was twisted slightly to her left, face in that direction also so that she was looking beyond me to where the book-sale volunteer had positioned himself in the chair.

Another staged, artificial situation communicating to me that I was virtually a non-person at the library, I recognized immediately. This one played out silently. No tone of scorn as with the previous one where the tall, thin volunteer asked me about what attention I was paying to current politics, more like a barking dog than one meaning to get an answer. No words at all. Instead as I looked at Cheryl, her head cocked and lips pursed to show dismay and disapproval at me being present in the main reading room of the Pequot Library, tolerated, yet scorned.

Wanting to take in the complete situation, I looked back to my right, to where Cheryl was looking, to the book-sale volunteer sitting in the chair. He was looking over to Cheryl nodding his head slightly, as if approving Cheryl's manifest distain, his lips too pursued, not so demonstrably as Cheryl's, yet intentionally copying her to affirm the shared bond between them. Having seen that I was getting the message of the staged incident by turning to see the man was looking back at Cheryl displaying the same look of annoyance over my presence, having come up from the basement when told I was in the library to impress it upon me, the volunteer got up from the chair, and walked from the room. Cheryl returned to behind the circulation desk. I looked back into the art book.

With Pequot Library's small staff, its limited area for library patrons and this all on one floor at that, and the popularity and easy accessibility of the library's children's area with residents of Southport and surrounding other parts of Fairfield and Westport, it wasn't long before Susan became identified with the children's library. As staff and patrons came to acknowledge, she was the children's librarian. Nearly all the time whenever children and ones with them would be at the children's area of the library, Susan would be there too.

But children and others wouldn't even have to go into the library to know Susan would be there. For in coming to the Library, even before they went in, they would see — could not miss seeing — Susan's dark metallic-green Honda SUV parked in the library parking lot which like the children's department of the library, became identified with her.

3. The FBI Targets the Pequot Library Executive Director

Among the varied roles of the Pequot Library executive director Heather-Marie
Montilla was encouraging individuals who were availing themselves of Pequot
Library's particular and in many ways unique facilities and environment to
continue to patronize the Library, to find it a welcoming place where they could
productively and reliably do the work or as with parents of children, fulfill the
purposes for which they patronized the library. It is not that the executive
director would become friends with particular patrons she recognized as regulars
and who such as me were always seen to be busy with some work tasks in line
with the facilities and environment the library offered to the public. But as with
me and others, Heather-Marie Montilla always presented a welcoming face, a
smiling nod or bright "hello." Occasionally Heather (as she was called by staff and
patrons) would have a brief stop with patron to remark on something in an
exhibition the patron was looking at or bring to a patron's attention something
new or forthcoming at the library she knew the patron was interested in.

Not long after being hired as executive director in October 2014, Heather
recognized me as a regular patron who was always seen to be busy with work
having to do with books, ephemera, and research on these. All the staff at the
circulation desk which overlooked the main reading room where I usually worked
when at the library and others coming and going in the public areas of the library
could see that I was doing something involved with books and related materials.
Staff working at the circulation desk overlooking the main reading room would
see me answer questions about books other patrons asked after they saw what I
was working on and that I was approachable, ready to help, and knowledgeable.
Sometimes a patron and I would have a short conversation about some particular
book he would show me or something to do with books and collecting or selling.
There was one regular patron who was actively buying older books and trying to
sell them for a profit I spoke with all the time when we were both at the library.

One time, an office worker seeing me standing at one of the computers which at
the time was in the hallway outside the office, came out to ask me about some
possession of hers. She wanted to know how she could find how much it was
worth. I told her how I and others involved in the antiques and auctions field did
basic pricing research using eBay. She could put a brief description of the item or
keywords applying to it into eBay's search box, and she would get returns on

similar items presently listed and prices for them, and could shift the search to similar items which had sold in recent months and their selling prices. Items which seemed they would have exceptional value would call for more detailed and skilled research, I advised her as well.

Robert Repko, whom I knew from high school and who was working as library custodian and overseer of books donated for the book sale, was another Pequot Library staff member who at times consulted me about books which had come in which appeared to have some special quality that would put them in the "specials" category of higher-priced books in the annual book sale. I learned that he was working at the library one day when he came up to me as I was working at my computer to let me know. I told him then I was in the book business, and it wasn't long before he started asking me questions about donated books he picked out he wanted me to appraise. A few times, Heather saw Robert Repko and I discussing something about a book he was showing me at a desk in the main reading room. She could not help but see and to overhear what we were talking about, and sometimes she paused as if to pick up a point or two about books and the book business.

Because I usually had a stack of books beside me when working at Pequot, the space for the public was limited, outside of the children's area limited to the main reading room and the couple of small rooms off of it, and there were usually no more than a few patrons in these areas at a time, I was easily recognized as someone involved with books. Needless to say, the primary interest of my occupation as well as a lifelong interest in books and an interest in books and what the library had to offer with regard to these with regular library patrons and library staff brought us together in varying ways and to varying degrees.

While I was at the 2015 Pequot Library Annual Book Sale in late July going through foreign-language books in rows along a table in the long, spacious tent set up in the parking lot for the sale, Heather, who was moving about the sale to see how it was going, spotted me, and came over to me. It was one of her friendly, welcoming gestures which I had by now become familiar with. The way she picked me out in particular and the distance she walked over to me indicated that it was something more than a routine, casual notice of a library regular. I took it as a kind of official "thank you" of me for being helpful and informative about books for patrons and library staff whenever asked something about books. I was a kind of resource for the library, a patron who readily and willingly participated in the library's interest and purpose of being known as a place where individuals could learn more about books and book culture. To some small degree, I was part of the good image the library liked to have, and Heather saw this.

It was only a couple of weeks later I found out that Heather was not the only person who had seen me in particular at the book sale; and I was not the only one who saw that Heather's coming over to me at the book sale was something more, something different than routine, perfunctory.

About a week later when I was in the main reading room sitting in a chair by the fireplace, Heather-Marie Montilla's recognition of me at the library was starkly different, signaling not only a new participant in the FBI's targeting of me at the Library, but also a new phase, a new level of targeting.

As small as the main reading room was and as attention-getting as Heather's movement was, Heather and I could not help seeing each other as she strode into the room. She seemed to hurry, though I could not surmise what for. Perhaps she hurried to get through the dislikable scene; perhaps someone was waiting on the phone in her office for her to return. But most likely — certainly — she hurried to create some distance between herself and the two younger women FBI agents coming behind her, as if to get away from them entirely.

This time, instead of a cheery greeting of a nod or "hello" which I had come to expect every time Heather's and my paths crossed at the library not long after she had become executive director, with her face in my general direction to her left as she moved along the length of the room, when she saw that I was looking back to politely, correspondingly respond to recognition of my presence or greeting from her, she then sharply held her left hand crooked at the elbow out from her to look down at her wrist as if looking at the time on a watch as explanation for her hurry and forgoing her usual manner toward me when we crossed paths at the library. In this incident, not only did she not give me the briefest glance directly, but her left arm had been interposed between us, like a barrier.

With the two women FBI agents trailing behind her, Heather went around behind me. The two agents were not moving so hurriedly as Heather. In the limited space, they didn't have to because Heather would never be far from them and would always be in their sight; and with no way out except the way they had come in, there was no way Heather would escape their accompanying her.

I didn't see where the trio went or what they did when they were behind me. I returned to my perusing of the day's newspaper. With Heather's markedly changed manner upon coming across me at the library and the two women FBI agents moving behind her, I recognized immediately that another FBI targeting incident was playing out before me, in the line of the ones previously involving the book-sale volunteers. Heather was not engaging with the two agents at all. It was evident that there was no library staff-patron relationship between them such as Heather responding to some inquiry or search by them, and doing so quickly to demonstrate efficiency and attentiveness. Heather did not engage with the agents by saying anything to them nor even looking back to see they were behind her. She knew that they would be behind her. Heather plodded through the staged targeting scenario virtually alone, turned from me and programmed.

I presume they went into the magazine room, one of the two small rooms off the main reading room, because of the time between when they slipped out of my sight moving behind me and when they again became visible to me.

I saw Heather first as she passed close to me to my right between me in the chair and the fireplace. Right behind her were the two agents. I didn't pay much attention since Heather's back was to me, and I presumed the three would move out of the reading room as suddenly as they had come into it. Yet at this point in this day's targeting, instead of moving past me as Heather had, the two agents stopped to my right. Standing close together, they were halfway turned to me, seeming to loom over me sitting in the low, roomy chair. I noticed them out of the corner of my eye, vague but certain presences.

I could see in my field of vision as my head instinctively partly raised in response to the two women FBI agents who stood over me less than a foot away in the narrow passage between the chair and the fireplace that Heather had stopped, and was looking back. She said something like, "That's our historic fireplace," as if the agents had stopped where they did to admire this feature of the historical, 1890's Pequot Library building even though the agents were not paying any attention to the fireplace, but had stopped close beside me to openly exert intimidation and to convey that the Pequot Library was now a location where I would be repeatedly targeted.

Although visibly unnerved by what the women FBI agents were putting her up to, the prolonged stop of the agents just beside me with their openly hostile look was too much for executive director Heather. Stopped and turned back to them, Heather looked pleadingly at them, imploring them to end the targeting which had gone on long enough for one incident and had served its purpose of informing me that I could no longer expect her to be friendly toward me at the library and that others, namely FBI agents which I realized even though Heather nor anyone else told me so, would be coming involved in library operations and with library staff. For Heather, it wasn't simply a matter of flouting decency, but also and more so a matter of her role and image as executive director and possible legal liability with respect to me as a patron and perhaps others if FBI agents were going to come into the library and intentionally disturb and harass them by targeting.

But decency, consideration for Heather or the Pequot Library, respect for individuals such as me or others, adverse legal ramifications, commission of crimes — none of this is of concern or even consideration for FBI people. Such sociopathy allows no reflection and thus knows no limits.

4. FBI Gang-Stalking/Social Cleansing at the Pequot Library, Southport

With the Pequot Library executive director openly taking part in the FBI targeting, book-sale volunteers coming into the main reading room to signal to me the FBI had involved them in the targeting, and other unusual incidents or scenarios I encountered for the first time in over three decades of patronizing the library such as an office worker sitting at a table in the main reading room staring at me when I entered it, children's librarian Susan Ei would surely know something was going on. Not only would she not have noticed unusual, different activity going on among the staff at times, but also, surely, with the library's small staff and regular conversation among it, she would have been told about the FBI's presence and activities.

Yet, aware of the FBI targeting activity and contact with different staff members to participate in it, from what I saw in August and September of 2015 when a particularly disturbing, menacing, and elaborated targeting incident took place, unlike the executive director, circulation desk employee Cheryl, and the book-sale volunteers, Susan's situation was that she was more aware of what was going on than a player in it. This is what I saw during the August 25, 2015, menacing incident involving multiple players who were FBI agents and Pequot Library staff working in concert that I describe as gang-stalking/social cleansing. The "gang-stalking" refers to the FBI's criminal mentality and tactics; the "social cleansing," to the FBI's program for shaping American society according to its preferences and designs. In August and September 2015, whatever Susan's awareness of the FBI's infiltration and enlistment of employees or her agreement with this, she was on the margins of this.

On August 25, 2015, about midday as I turned from Pequot Avenue onto Westway Road in Southport, Connecticut, to enter the driveway to the Pequot Library after having been to estate sales in western Fairfield County, I came upon to my left a dark-colored vehicle with its parking lights blinking. Since I often saw such vehicles with their lights on as I was out and around, such as when leaving my apartment parking lot or parking at the Southport post office to check mail, I saw this as one more such incident. Part of the FBI's silliness, I thought again, and its unconscionable, often criminal wastefulness.

I pulled into the library driveway, and parked to the right on part of the lawn seeing other vehicles were parked there. As I was getting out of my SUV, facing toward Pequot Avenue and generally in the direction of the larger-size black vehicle I had passed, I looked up to see if it was still parked where I had seen it. It was not. I saw it driving away to my left on Pequot Avenue.

In the Library, as was my habit, I went into the small room off the main reading room where the newspapers were kept to get the day's New York Times to photocopy the crossword puzzle. I liked to do this before getting down to work.

In the main room again, as I placed the newspaper down on one of the tables to pull out the Arts section with the crossword puzzle, a taller, black-haired woman came into view by the circulation desk. She was carrying an open laptop which was pointed toward me as she looked toward me. Thinking she was looking for a place to sit with her laptop, I picked up the sections of the New York Times I had been looking through for the Arts section, and while moving to the side of the table to clear the space, I spoke across to her something like, "I'm not sitting here. You can use this spot if you want." The woman did not answer, nor move toward me.

Getting no response, my attention turned to the newspaper. Pulling out the Arts section, I walked toward the photocopy machine. The woman with the laptop had been standing at a spot between me and it. She was no longer there as I moved to the copying machine.

As I placed the folded newspaper page with the crossword puzzle on the photocopy machine, the woman brought herself to my notice again. This time she was with Pequot Library public-relations director Adair Heitmann. The two women stood side-by-side off my right shoulder, slightly behind me.

As the two women stood near me, I heard Adair Heitmann say something like, "You can work downstairs if you want" or "Why don't you work downstairs." The woman however declined, saying something like no, she would work on this floor in the children's library so she could keep an eye on her children.

Once again recognizing that something odd was going on at the Pequot Library with respect to me, I looked to my left to see what was going on at this side. There I saw library employee Vickie Konopka, another longtime library staff member I knew. I was surprised to see Vickie since she is most of the time on the library's lower floor for her work. Vickie was mostly turned from me, but her face with a wide grin was turned back toward me.

I purposely looked past Vickie to see if any other individuals were at that side of me. Specifically I was looking to see if Susan Ei, the children's librarian, whose desk was a few yards from Vickie, was going to join the congregation collected around me. I saw Susan at her desk. She wasn't looking toward me, but rather paying attention to something on her desk. There was nothing abnormal nor suspicious about her location or appearance.

Running off the crossword puzzle and turning to my right to return to the main reading room, Adair Heitman and the black-haired woman she had been standing with had moved off. I didn't see either of them as I went back to the main reading room to return the day's newspaper where it was kept.

My next movement was to go to the room where the magazines were shelved to do the crossword puzzle and work at my laptop for a while. My first sight when I entered this room was a young man sitting in a chair facing me glaring menacingly at me. Not intending to be intimidated, I took another step or two into the room. Before I could get settled, a young Asian woman I had seen outside of the room came to me and told me that the room was to be used for some library-sponsored health event that would be starting shortly. Health products were displayed on a table set up below a set of windows outside the magazine room, as I had seen. The Asian woman asked me if I would like to take part, and I told her no, I had work to do.

I took a chair at the end of one of the long tables in the main reading room, near the shelves for newly-acquired books. This is a preferred seat for my computer work in my stops at the library because it is easy for me to get up and walk around a bit when I want to take a short break. The young man who had been glaring at me was now sitting in a chair about ten feet across from me facing me, still glaring menacingly. To his right was an older main, probably another FBI agent who was his trainer.

Quickly engaged in my computer work and not paying a lot of attention to what was going on elsewhere, in looking away from the computer at one time to give my eyes a rest and be somewhat refreshed for the next step of my task, for the third time in only a few minutes, I saw the tall, dark-haired woman who was an FBI agent. This time she was standing behind the circulation desk, behind library employee Denise Martin. Denise was looking out at me, the FBI woman agent standing with her back to me, but head turned sideways toward Denise. The agent and Denise were whispering to each other.

I looked back at my computer, and then around for a moment again as is my habit at my computer when I am not typing or looking at something on the screen. Glancing toward the circulation desk again only a moment later wondering if the woman might be a new library employee or at least getting a look at a new face in the library, I saw the woman still had her back to me, but was no longer leaning toward or whispering to Denise. She appeared to be doing something with her hands.

Not very curious about whatever was going on at the circulation desk because my only reason for having looked there was for a brief break from the computer screen, I turned back to my computer work. A moment later, as I was looking away from the screen again, I noticed the FBI agent had moved out from behind the circulation desk and was moving in my direction. I assumed she was going to see what was going on with the imminent health-related event. Two women who were together had passed by the table I was at in the direction of the magazine room. And I knew that library employees sometimes attended events in the Library.

I could not help but be generally aware of the movement of the FBI agent as one is intuitively aware of anyone moving around them. There was not much room behind me and the shelves of new books. The agent passed behind me. But as I saw out of the corner of my left eye half continuing to work at the computer and half naturally being aware of what was going on around me, I realized she was not continuing to the magazine room where the event was being held, but had stopped, and had turned to face where I was sitting at my computer.

A split second later, I heard the clicking of a camera on automatic. I recognized the sound from hearing this on TV crime shows when someone is being photographed by undercover agents, would-be assassins, private detectives, and such. I wasn't counting, but I would say six to eight photographs were taken of me in a period of three to four seconds.

Hearing the first and second metallic clicking of the agent's camera on automatic, I looked across the room slightly to my left. I wanted to see where the man who had been glaring menacingly at me was. I thought the camera might be a distraction so he could move into action to assault me. I think now maybe I was supposed to be provoked or frightened to lash out at or move aggressively toward the woman agent taking the photographs; and the male agent would then assault me or at least be a witness to aggressive behavior on my part.

The woman agent was no more than about two feet from me; the camera was aimed at me and clicking long enough for me to realize something was going on and then to realize what was going on; and the camera was being held close enough to my head—my left ear—to hear the series of fast metallic clicks clearly and be concerned if I might be struck with it since I was concentrating on the glowering man about ten feet from me while watching what was going on.

The woman agent moved back toward the circulation desk after taking the photographs automatically. There was no indication she had come to this spot in the library close to me for any reason other than harassing and disturbing me and trying to startle or alarm me to take some sudden, reflexive movement which would be interpreted as "violent," thus confirming the FBI's justification for targeting me that I was an aggrieved individual prone to violence.

I didn't see where the woman FBI agent went. No longer so concerned about the glowering man sitting in the chair not far from me, I got back to my computer tasks. I stayed at the library a bit longer, then left.

With its complex organization and precise timing, the number of players including multiple FBI agents and Pequot Library employees, the alarming intensity and virulence of the woman FBI agent's wielding her camera at me, and the objective to startle me into a seemingly violent reaction (an oft-used law-enforcement technique) evidenced new dimensions of the FBI targeting of me. I wasn't the only one who had to deal with new circumstances coming out of the gang-stalking/social cleansing incident however. By visibly remaining on the sidelines, taking no assigned role, taking part in no trickery of me, and manifesting no hostility toward me, Susan Ei had made herself a target of the FBI. Susan's sense of common decency, understanding that the Pequot Library, like any library, was for patrons' use, enjoyment, and peace, her knowledge of my involvement with books and book culture, her long-time acquaintance with me as a Library regular, and her inbred values and ideals marked her as a target for the FBI. In the FBI's eyes, with her resistance of the FBI depravity whatever form and whatever strength, this resistance, however faint or tentative or provisional it might be, made Susan a target as much as my exposures of FBI crime and corruption, mocking of its presumptions as a "premier" law-enforcement agency made up of "special" agents, and descriptions of its activities that are at once clownish, menacing, and stupid made me a target.

That unlike the smarmy Denise Martin, the duplicitous Adair Heitmann, Susan Ei did not immediately and totally succumb to FBI wishes and instructions and did not commit herself to a role however minor or tangential if only for the sake of deference to the FBI, like me, Susan was seen as an obstruction to the FBI's megalomania and totalitarian, pathological ambitions of population control.

5. The Cover-Up Begins

After the 2015 Labor Day went by, in the morning of September 15, I sent to Heather-Marie Montilla and selected Pequot Library staff including Susan Ei as children's librarian a 1500-word email giving them background on the August 25 FBI planned and executed gang-stalking/social cleansing incident. The background — and in fact motive — for the FBI targeting of me is my filing a criminal complaint against Pullman and Comley law firm lawyers James T. Shearin and Timothy A. Bishop for theft of about $6,000 of medical films of mine and filing and winning a civil case against Connecticut state's attorneys for an illegal wiretap on my phone. Yes, you read that right: The FBI originally targeted me for taking lawful actions against individuals who had committed crimes against me. The targeting started about 2012.

The FBI's targeting of me was related to the FBI's affinity with Hillary Clinton as 2016 Democratic presidential candidate against Donald Trump, and the fact that Connecticut is a deep blue state with Democratic governor Dannell Malloy who was a Clinton favorite expected to be given a Cabinet position in a Clinton presidency. The targeted of me was an aspect of the "Russian conspiracy" charade perpetrated by the FBI in trying to undermine Trump's campaign and smear individuals who were part of it. Apolitical for the most part, I was not a supporter of Trump or involved in anything to get him elected president. Nonetheless, the FBI targeted me because of Malloy's relationship with Clinton and the Pullman and Comley law firm's relationship with Malloy. The Pullman and Comley law firm was a major contributor to the state Democratic Party, and was Malloy's favorite law firm.

That afternoon, I got a message on my iPhone answering service from a Fairfield police officer. Pequot Library executive director had contacted the Fairfield police about my email to her and selected staff, and an officer wanted to talk to me about it. I called back, spoke with officer Joseph Kalson, and said I would be down to the police department soon to discuss the matter.

When I got to the station, the officer led me into a small room off the lobby of the headquarters. He sat down across from me with a copy of my email laid in front of him. As I sat across from Kalson, he told me that the library executive director Heather-Marie Montilla had told him to tell me that neither she nor the library wanted to be involved in any political matter or differences between me and individuals and organizations I had noted in my email were behind the FBI infiltration of the library and contacts with Library employees and were responsible for the alarming August 25, 2015, incident targeting me as a library patron. Officer Kalson also informed me that executive director Heather-Marie Montilla wanted me to no longer have any contact with her.

When I told the police officer the reason for my email to the executive director and other upper-level staff at the Library — namely, the August 25 incident which I regarded as threatening — he said that I should have notified people at the library about it. When he said this, I replied, "Why should I do that? They already knew about it. The woman came out from behind the circulation desk." The "woman" I was referring to as the officer knew since I had just mentioned her in my sketch of the incident was the one who had menaced me by thrusting the camera at me and tried to provoke an incident in which I could have been seriously injured.

"She came out from behind the desk?", the officer questioned, more in disbelief than a question.

"Yes," I told him.

As soon as he heard this, the officer got up and left the room. I followed him out, not knowing what I was supposed to do. I watched him leave the lobby into the off-limits front desk area of the headquarters, and I left.

That whoever the Fairfield police officer had been in contact with at the Pequot Library had not mentioned the incident giving rise to my email and that the officer quickly left the room after I told him that the Pequot Library was complicit in the incident in some way disclosed the elements of the situation at the Library. The Fairfield police officer and by extension the Fairfield police department were not disposed to investigate wrongdoing at the Pequot Library. It was't long before I was described as "disturbed" in police reports as matters unfolded in the coming couple of weeks. As for the Pequot Library, the cover-up of any wrongdoing or crimes toward me as a patron had already begun.

On September 18, 2015, in the early afternoon, about 1:30 pm, after going to a Norwalk estate sale, I stopped at the library to use the men's room and if the opportunity presented itself, try to find out the name of the unknown woman in the August 25 targeting incident whom Adair Heitmann by standing close to me had wanted me to know had some relationship with the library and who had been standing beside Denise Martin at the circulation desk. I also wanted to get the name of a contact at the library or individual associated with it I could contact regarding a lawsuit I would be initiating against the library since it was my understanding according to what Fairfield police office Kalson had told me, executive director Heather Marie Montilla did not want me to have any contact with her.

Parking in the part of the parking lot along side the Library, turning from shutting the door after getting out, I saw Adair Heitmann about fifteen yards away strolling along the edge of the lot. I saw this could be an opportunity to find the name of the unknown woman I was hoping to find and also the name of an individual at the library or representing it to be in touch with regarding my impending legal actions.

As I approached Adair plainly wishing to speak with her, recognizing me, she said "hello," and stopped. I responded, and asked her if it were alright to have a word with her. She was agreeable.

I said to her that as I knew she had been associated with the library for some time and she held the position of publicist and public-relations director, maybe she could give me the information I was looking for. I first asked her if she knew the name of the woman she had been standing with at a previous stop of mine at the library.I didn't mention the August 25 date since I didn't think this would mean anything to her. Instead, I related details to jog Adair's recollection and specify the woman I was referring to. I told her that this would be the woman she had been standing with the time I was at the copy machine and the two were close to me over my right shoulder; the woman to whom Adair had asked if she would like to work downstairs, but the woman replied that she would work on this floor, the main floor, in the children's section so she could keep an eye on her children. Adair chuckled. "Oh...oh...you know...I meet so many people here," she said airily.

Rebuffed by Adair concerning the name of the unknown woman, I moved right on to the matter of a library staff member or representative such as a lawyer I could be in contact with concerning legal matters I would be pursuing against the library. I mentioned to her that I was seeking such a representative because I had been told by a Fairfield Police officer that Heather-Marie Montilla did not want me to contact her after having received a lengthy email from me. Adair replied that she didn't know who such a staff member or representative would be. She said if I had a business card I could give her, she would see that it got to the right person, and that person would be in touch with me. I took out my wallet and pulled out a business card of my bookselling business, and handed it to Adair.

My brief encounter with Adair ended, I turned and walked away to go into the library to use the men's room. Passing through the tall swinging doors with cut-glass panels, turning to the left and coming upon the circulation desk as I had to to get to the stairs leading down to the men's room, I saw Denise Martin was at the desk. Coming along the hallway toward the desk was Susan Ei.

I stopped to speak to Denise Martin. I wanted to see if she would give me the name of the taller, dark-haired woman she had been whispering with some days ago. I don't remember if I got to ask or had asked and Denise had not said anything. For unbeknownst to me, Adair had followed closely behind me into the library, and abruptly appeared beside me urgently and insistently telling Denise, "No one is to speak to this man." By this time, Susan Ei, seeing that something was going on having to do with the August 25 incident, the FBI woman agent having a leading part in it, and library employees who took part in it, had wheeled around and was decidedly striding away from the scene. I watched her back for the first few steps she took.

Adair Heitmann was so alarmed and making such a commotion commanding that Denise Martin and I suppose Susan Ei too whom she had seen approaching the circulation desk that I drew back a little. I had't expected to get the name of the woman anyway, but was just taking a try; and Adair Heitmann had told me she would pass on my request to get a contact connected to the Library, so I felt I had accomplished something. From my left, Adair leaned partly across the front of me, as if spreading herself on the top of the circulation desk, putting herself between me and Denise Martin. Adair Heitmann was agitated, alarmed, worried. It would make no sense for me to make any attempt to challenge her dictum that no one speak to me. There would be plenty of time for speaking about all sorts of things later, when my lawsuit was underway. So I didn't say anything or press the matter in any way, but immediately went down the stairway behind the circulation desk to the downstair's men's room.

When I came up the stairs a minute or two later, I turned left toward the library offices at the end of the short hallway and the children's library area to the left of them. I wanted to see if the unknown dark-haired woman who had menaced me in late August happened to be in the library that day.

At the end of the hallway, I turned left to look in the children's section. Glancing around quickly, I saw no taller, dark-haired woman. Friday afternoon on a nice sunny, early fall day, the children's area was empty except for Susan Ei, who was now sitting at her desk.

I then turned to retrace my steps and leave the library quickly since I hadn't planned to stay for work that day. Taking a few steps, I came upon executive director Montilla. She was holding the business card I had given to Adair in the driveway in front of her with both hands, looking down at it. With Heather displaying my business card and standing still in front of me where I could not help but come near her on my way out, it was obvious she wanted to speak with me. I wondered why she was placing herself where I would have to come close to her and also why she was indicating she wanted me to stop and have words with her since the Fairfield police officer Joseph Kalson had told me Heather had told him to inform me that she wanted no further contact with me.

I stopped in any event. Of course, Heather wanted to speak about the serious legal matters concerning the library I had raised with Adair Heitmann in my brief encounter with her in the parking lot, and which it was obvious Adair had related to her when giving Heather my business card. In fact at some point in the encounter involving Heather and me lasting two to three minutes, Heather expressed that she was the library director, and anything concerning the library was of interest to her. When she said this, I replied that this was my understanding.

I do not remember the order of the varied subjects Heather and I went over in our short encounter, which was something like a conversation. However, as I recall, I expect I first informed Heather that the library was facing what I regarded as serious legal matters entailed criminal accusations against certain library staff regarding multifaceted and conspiratorial hostile acts against me in the Pequot Library not long ago. At one point, Heather began to apologize for a "rude" treatment of me by anyone connected with the Library. I cut her off saying that events had moved beyond the point of an apology resolving the situation; and besides, what I experienced was not rudeness, but overt, explicit, coordinated, unmistakable, and intentionally fear-inducing hostility. I explained to Heather than while at the Library that day mainly to use the men's room, I was seeing if I could find out the name of the unknown taller, black-haired woman who had been involved in the menacing, etc., of me; and also find out the representative for the library regarding the legal actions I would be pursuing since I had heard from the Fairfield police department that she did not want me to contact her on these matters.

I told Heather that I was on the verge of filing a criminal complaint, initiating a civil case, and publicizing the hostile incident at the library and my accusations regarding library staff members. My interchange with Heather ended with an agreement between us that by the coming Wednesday—September 23, 2015—she would be in touch with me with the name and contact information of the individual to represent the library regarding the legal issues and possibly related matters I was informing her about. I suggested to Heather that I believed one or more board members were lawyers, and they could probably give her guidance under the circumstances.

At one point in our conversation, Heather told me she hadn't been director that long. I knew this as I am aware of and in fact follow situations and developments at the Pequot Library. I advised Heather that I thought she was being taken advantage of because of her relative newness in the position of director, a position she was still learning about and becoming familiar with. I also advised Heather that the FBI cared nothing about her, saying the FBI just wanted to get me and implying the FBI cared nothing about any of the other staff of the library, or the patrons either, or the image, activities, and role and place of the library in the community.

On my way out of the library by the front door where I had come in and which was the closest to where I had parked, I strode around the main room looking in the magazine room and the room where newspapers are kept to see if by chanceA No-Trespass the unknown woman or the man who had been scowling at me in the August 25, 2015, menacing incident were in either. No one was in either room. Then I left the Library hurriedly since I had stayed much beyond the short time I had expected. I wanted to get to the Fairfield Public Library to look for movie DVDs for the weekend and do some reading of periodicals.

6. A No-Trepass Order, a Lawsuit Filed, Death Threats, and the Beginnings of the Stalking

Because of the no-trespass order, the Pequot Library would no longer be a location where I could be targeted by FBI planned and perpetrated disturbing and threatening incidents. However, as the FBI had found in its infiltration and enlistment of diverse employees, the Pequot Library had proved to be fertile ground for accomplices willing to participate in its schemes and crimes.

Two days or so after Fairfield police officer Chanse Wilkie had told me that I was barred from the Pequot Library under threat of arrest for trespass in mid September 2015, as I was sitting in a chair at the Fairfield Public Library, Robert Repko, Pequot Library custodian and high-school classmate from the 1960s, made his presence know to me by walking across an open area of the library in my line of sight. My head jerked as a was startled, taken aback.

In more than fifty years of patronizing the Fairfield Public Library and spending time there three or four times a week during this time, usually about two hours a time, I had never seen Robert Repko there. Besides, I knew he lived in Southport, not more than two or three minutes from the Pequot Library; and from my talks with him and from overhearing his chats with other employees, I knew that he patronized Pequot for checking out books he was interested in reading and other typical services of a library. Since his reading tastes were mainstream, Pequot Library would have the types of books he read.

Furthermore, Robert Repko liked to fancy himself that he was rubbing elbows with the elite by being employed at the Pequot Library. This was the draw of working at the library for most of its employees. Although Southport has middle class areas, it is widely known for its fabulous wealth. The Pequot Library is in the area of Southport of its large old houses or modern-era ones which have replaced them, all having impressively landscaped yards and priced in the millions. To emphasize that he was worthy of this moneyed elite, Robert Repo drove a Mercedes the two or three minutes it took him to get to and from the Pequot Library for his work as custodian. At one of the annual books sales I was talking to a dealer as we waited to get numbers to get into the sale when it opened the following day, Robert Repko pulled into the Library driveway with his Mercedes. He and I waved to each other. "Who's that?", the dealer i was talking to asked.

"The custodian," I replied. The dealer wheezed. "Pretty ritzy," he said, "Even the custodians have Mercedes." Southport was synonymous with wealth.

Robert Repko saw when I saw him striding across the open area of the Pequot Library. I looked at him out of politeness to at least acknowledge his presence as I would have anywhere I saw him. But Robert did not look directly back. Though he walked in my direction and his face was toward me, his eyes were cast beyond me, as if looking off into the distance with a swirling mix of embarrassment and fear. He moved past me quickly, wanting to get the scenario over as quickly as possible, acknowledging me only by making certain by his positioning of himself and his ostentatious striding that I would see him and would know that he was enacting an incident of targeting which would bring to my mind the vicious, threatening targeting incident at the Pequot Library not long ago.

But Robert Repko, library custodian, overseer of the book-sale volunteers who worked in the basement, and high-school classmate from some 50 years ago, was not the FBI's biggest prize for its plans to exponentially build on what it had created at the Pequot Library. The Pequot Library was both a resource for defamation and demonization of me with employees making false statements about me to Fairfield police and anyone else who would listen and pool for actors in targeting incidents wherever I was.

When Fairfield police officer Chanse Wilkie told me in September 2015 in the lobby of the Fairfield police headquarters I would be arrested for trespass if I went to the Pequot Library again, I told him that I had every intention of returning to the Pequot Library, "Do you want to arrest me now?," I said to him. Officer Wilkie said that I would have to be at the Pequot Library to get arrested.

In doing research about my legal options in having in effect been framed for troubling Pequot Library employees and what would happen upon getting arrested for trespass at the Library and how this would play out, I ran across a comment at one website that it was better to be a plaintiff in a civil case than a defendant in a criminal case. This made sense to me. So after research on grounds for a civil case against the Pequot Library and certain employees, on March 7, 2016, I filed a civil case against the Pequot Library, different employees including Adair Heitmann and Denise Martin, and the library Board of Trustees.

With the FBI monitoring my computer as a part of its targeting of me, they knew from my research and from my development of my complaint that a lawsuit against the library and other defendant was a certainty, and that the lawsuit would be filed before long. Knowing this, the FBI made two death threats against me. The first was on February 6, 2016. This death threat was a military-style baseball cap with a death's head insignia on it and also the number of a military unit. The cap with the skull covering its crown was placed outside the door of my apartment on a chest-high cardboard box the tenant across the hall from me had outside the door of his apartment, with the death's head facing me where I could not help seeing it as I stepped out of my apartment. I posted a photo of this cap with the death's head on Facebook.

I got the second death threat on February 25. This threat was red blotches looking like blood stains, or perhaps actual blood, on the complaint against Pequot Library that the clerk's office at the Bridgeport Superior Court on Main Street had sent me upon my fee waiver request that filing fees of hundreds of dollars be waived. With debt payments and most of my income going for business expenses, my net income was low enough so that I qualified for a fee waiver for the lawsuit.

The death threats were the FBI's opening signs that the targeting would escalate and intensify. The FBI was not concerned about the Pequot Library employee defendants and the board members backing up the employees' false, malicious statements about me. The FBI wanted to ensure that its own malevolent infiltration of the Pequot Library as part of its overall targeting regimen of me and the associated involvement of library employees would not come to light. With the number of employees the FBI had involved over a few months and knowing by now that I was to some degree determinedly and effectively exposing the FBI crimes and corruption, the FBI began to interfere with and obstruct my legal and publishing activities now focusing on the outrageous August 2015 Pequot Library targeting incident that was especially alarming for me.

Susan Ei became involved in this period of the targeting of me after my lawsuit against the library and the others had been filed.

The first incident signaling to me that Susan Ei was no longer going to be sitting on the sidelines of the FBI determined, systematic, extensive targeting occurred in the Southport post office. I've had a post office box in Southport since the 1980s when I started different self-employed activities, desktop publishing, freelance writing, and consulting among these. I'd usually stop two or three times a week to check mail; and it was at these times when I was in Southport only about a quarter mile from the Pequot Library, I would stop there for a while too.

In late March 2016, about three weeks after I had filed my case against the Pequot Library and others and following the death threats of the cap with the death's head insignia outside the door of my apartment and the red blotches looking like blood on a document sent to me from the Bridgeport Superior Court's clerk's office, Susan Ei made an abrupt and brief appearance in the Southport post office. As was standing last in the line of a few persons waiting for one of the clerks attending the counters to be free, Susan came through the door with a large pane of glass between the lobby and the room with the counters where I was standing. I hadn't seen her come in. I wasn't paying attention to anything in particular as I waited, but off and on looked behind me to pass the time to see if anyone else would be taking a place in line. I might have to move forward a little since there wasn't much space in this room.

Susan pulled up close to me, about an arm's length away. She had come into the room so abruptly, I didn't notice her come in. The first I noticed her was when I glanced behind me — and there she was, standing close and facing me, but not looking at me. She had a blank look on her face. Assured that I had seen her, she then turned and left the room as abruptly as she had come in.

It was evident to me Susan had come into the post office only to be seen by me. We had never run across each other at the Southport post office in the thirty or so years I had been going there to check mail at my post office box. Once Susan was certain that I had seen her standing close beside me after I looked directly at her and gave her a look of recognition prepared to respond to a greeting should one come, she turned, and strode out.

I didn't dwell on the odd incident. I had become used to strange behavior by staff of the Pequot Library. Yet that there was an association between Susan's odd appearance and odd behavior, the August 2015 targeting incident of me, the death threats related to the forthcoming filing of my lawsuit against the library and some staff members, and the actual filing of it in early March 2016 came naturally to my mind. Along with the association with these other experiences, I also had thoughts that someone would have told Susan I was at the post office so she could then come in to engage in the simple scenario the FBI had designed for her.

The second Susan Ei stalking incident took place at the Southport post office too. This was about mid April 2016. Again I was standing last in line waiting for a postal clerk to get free. And again Susan made an appearance unnoticed by me at first, again quickly and obviously intentionally coming to me and standing close to me, again facing me with blank look on her face.

This scenario overall occurring in mid April was prolonged and somewhat elaborated, while still remaining basically simple and decidedly odd. After being certain that I had seen her, Susan, as before, abruptly left without saying a word or showing the slightest flicker of recognition, except for finding where I was standing and the moving like an automaton to stand right beside me.

Finishing my business with the postal clerk, pushing open the door between the front lobby and the room with the counters where customers stood in line, to my surprise, Susan Ei was there waiting for me, as I saw as soon as I opened the door and stepped from the area with the counters. Susan was standing to my right, having taken the same pose of body fully facing me with face slightly angled and eyes looking off into space, a by now familiar appearance when I came across FBI stooges of simultaneously making it clear I was being targeted by movement and body language signaling this while at the same time studiously seeming to ignore me to convey that I was a nonperson. This is one of the mechanics of the FBI's activity of ostracization, a concept of continual amusement to me for the FBI's presumption that it is somehow invested with the moral qualities, the respectable values, or the intelligence to make judgments on such a matter. The FBI is a menace to all for its clod-like mindset and moral blindness, but it is also funny in many ways.

Susan Ei having moved out of line to position herself so I would come upon her facing me standing like a stone on my way out of the post office confirmed her purpose was to target me if there had been any doubt at all. Having left the line waiting for a clerk to free up, but not leaving the building, and having taken the position she did in the lobby knowing I would be coming out of the counter area soon and would have to pass her on the only way out, she made plain that she had not come to the post office for some mailing task.

In this second encounter with Susan, I was carrying some mail that had been in my post office box which I cleaned out before having stood in line. As was my habit, I stood at a wide, five-foot long, waist-high table to my left for customer use to open envelopes and small parcels. In doing this, my back was to Susan. Curious as I was going through my mail, I glanced around two or three times to see if she was still there, in the spot where I had seen her. I knew she hadn't left the building since I would have noticed her to my right going out the front door. What I was curious about was if Susan was remaining where she had positioned herself where I would see her in coming out of the room with the counter. Each times I glanced around, there was Susan standing in the same spot.

She did leave before I finished going through my mail. I didn't see her outside when I left after finishing my post office tasks for the day. The two encounters with Susan that day I was at the Southport post office added nothing to what I had already come to realize upon the first encounter. The FBI had gotten to Susan, and she was now in their hands.

7. The Stalking Extended

The third stalking incident was at a different location. It extended the range of the stalking, and added another actor.

Harry's Wine and Liquor Market was about three quarters of a mile east of the Southport post office, along the Post Road between Southport and my apartment in the Black Rock section of Bridgeport. Convenient for me and a well-stocked wine shop with a knowledgable staff, I stopped there two or three times a month to buy some wine. As the FBI knew.

As at the Southport post office, in my decades of going to Harry's, I had never seen Susan Ei there. But one day she was there. She had followed me in after I had parked in the lot. This was in early May 2016. I know this because when I first passed the spot where she was standing when I saw her, she hadn't been there. Not seeing any employee at the register to my right as I entered Harry's, I continued to the area at the back of the store where the larger bottles of wine I usually buy are displayed. From this spot, I looked around to see what staff were present and if there were any other customers. I didn't see any staff, nor any other customers. It was early afternoon, a quiet time for the shop. I did see Susan, however, standing by the cash register at the front counter, looking toward me. She must have been in the parking lot waiting in the event I did stop at Harry's that day. It had taken me only seconds between entering the shop and getting to the place at the back wall. Though I didn't see Susan until I looked around from there, she had to have been only seconds behind me to have entered and taken the place where I first saw her.

Standing next to the front counter, Susan was staring at me over the rows of wine bottles on display in racks. After seeing her, I went about looking among the 1.5 liter bottles standing along shelves in the back of the shop. I continued looking, but looked around again to see what Susan was doing this time. Nothing different at this point — same pose facing me registering that she had picked me out and was seeing me, same blank stare on her face. I had looked around the second time to see if there was any indication Susan had come into Harry's for any other reason than that I was there. There wasn't any indication. Unmoving, Susan stared off in my direction, motionless, as if lifeless.

I didn't yet pick out a bottle to purchase. I left this place in the store, and walked in Susan's direction, though not straight toward her. Even though I could have moved directly to the other side of the shop, I purposely made a looping path to it. For about halfway along this path, Susan was in my view at different points to my right. I didn't come closer than about ten feet from her. I didn't try to evoke any response from her. I was trying to see what would happen.

In the other side of the store, I stood next to a stack of beer cartons, in front of me single bottles of beer in the cooler. I wanted to make sure I was still visible to Susan, but in a different spot. Sure enough, when I looked from this spot to Susan, she had turned so she was facing me while not moving from the spot she had taken when she had first come into the shop.

While looking ahead as if looking at the bottles of beer in the cooler, suddenly to my right a man striding hastily came into view. He passed about a foot in front of me, almost brushing against me.

Having had enough of the scene, I went back to the place with the 1.5 liter bottles by the direct path. I quickly selected one. When I turned to go to the front counter taking me right toward where Susan had been standing, she was gone. So was the man who had walked quickly and energetically in front of me. This time, Susan had been accompanied by an FBI agent.

After the three, there were no more stalking incidents involving Susan. But his was not the end of her FBI-directed presence in my life.

I mentioned Susan's distinctive metallic-green Honda SUV earlier. She was identified with this. It was a bright olive green, one of the larger Honda SUV models. Susan wasn't a showoff, nor ostentatious. The metallic-green SUV that seemed to glow and couldn't be ignored when parked in the Pequot Library parking lot or anywhere else related to her sense of individuality and was a tame, inoffensive idiosyncrasy. It went along with her creativity of a kind which made her an outstanding, effective, and appreciated children's librarian for the Pequot Library.

In its targeting with the intent of inducing fear and sense of constant threat in the target, the FBI devises encounters with individuals by agents or accomplices and sometimes sightings of objects which would have a special meaning for the target which to outside observers can be chalked off as normal happenstances or coincidences. When a target points to such encounters or objects as evidence of the FBI targeting and often correspondingly to a skeptic tries to explain how he knows such are evidence, his sanity and emotional state are usually questioned. I've been called "paranoid" more times than I can remember. Once the judge in a hearing said that my claims of legal malpractice, theft, and related others against lawyers at the Pullman and Comley law firm who had stolen medical films of mine made me look "paranoid." I replied, "If I weren't paranoid, I never would have been able to figure it out."

The treachery of lawyer criminals, FBI agents, spousal abusers, and other antisocial psychopaths entails such seemingly ordinary scenarios which to the ones involved in them, both target and the ones doing the targeting, are actually menacing incidents which by their repetition induce a sense of fear, uncertainty, and vulnerability in the target. I call this the "semiotics of terrorism." As with the FBI in its practices in pursuit of population control, this semiotics of fear is practiced in totalitarian societies on a large scale. As the inhabitants of totalitarian countries are kept in a state of constant fear and apprehension by practices of the state, so are targets of the FBI kept in a state of constant fear and apprehension by similar FBI practices. In America, the closer government practices and FBI practices come to reflect each other and merge together, the greater the threat to American democracy. Targets are not only individuals such as myself who are unscrupulously made targets by the FBI and who are identified as targets to others by FBI defamation and demonization, but individuals such as Susan Ei, who was targeted to be a part of the FBI's program of threatening me by semiotics of fear.

I wasn't startled when one day coming out of my apartment and rounding the back of my gray Honda CR-V to put my computer on the driver's seat, I came upon Susan Ei's characteristic dark green metallic Honda SUV parked in a parking space of an adjacent apartment building owned by the same landlord. By this time, I was well aware of the perverse, pathetic stunts of the FBI and its total control over individuals such as Susan Ei the FBI had targeted as accomplices.

Susan Ei's Honda SUV was facing me diagonally about 15 feet away across an open space at one end of the building, as motionless and silently as she had faced me in the three stalking incidents. There was no chance Susan would have driven her Honda to the Black Rock area of Bridgeport where I lived. Among residents of Fairfield and other affluent towns in Fairfield County, Bridgeport had a terrible reputation, especially with women. Women would not come to Bridgeport — they were fearful. Moreover, there was nothing in the area where Susan's SUV was parked for her to come to it. There were no shops, no homes with genteel woman Susan might want to visit, no connection to her position or activities as children's librarian of Pequot Library. Susan's Honda SUV parked outside my apartment building was the FBI's way of conveying to me as an instance of its characteristic semiotics of terrorism that the August 2015 gang-stalking/social cleansing incident at the Pequot Library was the origination of a much wider activity of menacing and harassment, and also that the FBI had not only Susan Ei but also many others who would be involved in this activity at any place and any time.

Susan's Honda was parked in the same parking space by my parking space at my apartment building two more times. The third time it was there, I took a photo of it with my iPhone. That was the last time it was there.

8. My Lawsuit Against Susan Ei

On the first day of December 2016, I started a civil case against Susan Ei for invasion of privacy, defamation, and emotional distress at the Bridgeport Superior Court on Main Street. (FBT-CV16-5032337-S) About a week later, the case was removed to District Federal Court in an attempt by Susan's lawyers to combine the case with the case I had going against the Pequot Library and individuals associated with it growing out of the August 2015 targeting incident. I objected to the removal on the grounds that my case against Susan concerned different claims at different locations at different times. Susan did not begin stalking me in league with the FBI until near the end of March 2016 whereas the Pequot Library case was based on incidents at the Pequot Library in August and September 2015. That the stalking coincided with my initiating a case against the Pequot Library and other defendants was apparent. But the Susan Ei case filed in December 2016 was not integrally involved with the incidents, defendants, or claims of the Pequot Library case filed in March 2016.

With my objection, I submitted an affidavit stating that I had no evidence that Susan Ei had participated in the August 25, 2015, incident. In fact, as I stated, I had evidence that she hadn't. At the time the incident was unfolding at the Pequot Library, I had seen Susan sitting at her desk going about her normal business. And when I had gone to the Pequot Library on September 18 to get the name of someone to be in touch with regarding my impending lawsuit against the library and had stopped at the front desk to have a word with Denise Martin, Susan Ei, quickly grasping my reason for being there, turned on her heels and strode away. My objection sustained by a Federal judge, my case against Susan Ei was remanded to state court, the Bridgeport Superior Court in March 2017. The date recorded for this by the Bridgeport Superior Court's clerk's office is March 29, 2017. The date of the Federal judge's ruling is March 27, 2019. However, in following this case in District Federal Court with PACER (the Federal court docket system standing for Public Access to Court Electronic Records), I learned that remand to state court had been ordered on March 9, with March 24 given as the date the case had gone through the administrative process and been officially remanded.

Knowing that my case against Susan Ei had been ordered remanded, I filed an amended complaint in the Bridgeport court's clerk's office.

According to Connecticut civil case procedure, a plaintiff can file an amended complaint up to thirty days following the filing of an original complaint initiating a case. This had been my practice in relation to requesting fee waivers for the fee filing a case. At the time, this cost was about $350, an expense I was not willing to take on after being cheated in previous cases by perjurious affidavits, corrupt judges, and other subversion, and with my business expenses and debt payments, my net income was low enough that I qualified for a fee waiver.

I kept my original complaints to be served by a state marshal simple because a marshal charges one dollar for copying each page of a complaint, multiplied by the number of defendants to be served as called for. Since earlier civil cases of mine had multiple defendants, copying costs for complaints could get costly. Hence, my simplified complaints in my first step of starting a law suit.

My first complaint served to Susan Ei by a state marshal was five pages for five counts not going into specifics or detail on the series of stalking incidents and Susan permitting her Honda SUV to be used in the FBI carrying its threats to me virtually to my doorstep. My second complaint was eleven pages for seven counts. In it, I went into detail on each of the three stalking incidents and the threat of Susan's vehicle parked outside my apartment similar to what I wrote earlier. Although I did nothing more than relate what I had witnessed and Susan knew what she had done, seeing her tawdry, uncharacteristic, threatening actions in the public document of my amended complaint posted at the case docket log of the Connecticut judicial website was a shock. It ripped through her like a savage dog. She had opened herself to the malignancy and predation of the FBI, and to its attendant parasitism. The ruthless savagery of the FBI ravaged her, eroded her sense of self, and ultimately devoured her.

I never understood Susan Ei's extreme reaction to seeing her transgressions made public. She knew that I had filed lawsuits against individuals at the Pequot Library involved in what I regarded as serious assaults against me. She knew FBI intimidation of me including death threats were not deterring me from publicizing on social media and in emails what I saw not only as threats to me, but assaults on and subversion of democratic civil society. She knew that I had pursued a case against the prominent Pullman and Comley law firm and its lawyers James T. Shearin and Timothy A. Bishop who had stolen medical films of mine meant for an operation on my neck. She knew that I was ridiculing, criticizing, and exposing powerful individuals in Connecticut including governor Malloy, judges, and state's attorneys. She knew these things because I had mentioned or alluded to them in an email to the library executive director and higher-level staff including her at the Pequot Library following the August 2015 gang-stalking/social cleansing incident, and because Pequot Library staff were following my postings on social media.

Susan Ei and all Pequot Library staff and also board members knew the Pequot Library FBI infiltration and related targeting incident of me were not the only FBI actions against me, and the Pequot Library situation was not unique nor isolated. How it is that Susan Ei or any other individual at the Pequot Library would think they were isolated or immune from my legal, publication, and exposure activities is something I do not understand. I attribute such recklessness on the part of Susan Ei to the recklessness of the FBI in recruiting her, as the FBI was reckless and indifferent in recruiting others connected to the Library. Susan Ei however proved to have vulnerabilities others did not — emotional, psychological, and medical vulnerabilities.

9. Susan Ei Becomes a Target of the FBI

Susan Ei was not prepared for exposure. I have no idea why she was not foreseeing this. While she had not been a participant in the FBI's vicious, alarming gang-stalking/social cleansing targeting incident of me at the Pequot Library in August 2015, she undoubtedly was aware of this. And she would have observed the stage of it at the copy machine where library employee Adair Heitmann and the taller, black-haired FBI agent played out the ruse that the agent was recognized as someone who had a special association with the library since this was in a straight line of view from where Susan Ei was sitting at her desk in the children's area of the library.

After my first step in being frank and communicative with the executive director and others at the Pequot Library was taken as cause for barring me from the Library with a no-trespass order delivered by the Fairfield police, I began publicizing what had gone on, identifying by name different individuals I recognized had been part of the FBI scheme. I never mentioned Susan Ei at this point. Nor was Susan included as a defendant among the multiple defendants in my civil case initiated in early 2016. Yet Susan knew that I was not hesitant about identifying individuals by name and describing what I regarded not only as significant, disturbing, ominous hostilities toward me involving multiple individuals instigated, planned, and carried out by FBI agents, but also significant transgressions of social norms and reflections of much larger, more extensive FBI crimes and corruption and intentions.

Susan Ei should have had no doubt that I would be naming her and describing her actions should she become visibly, disturbingly, and ominously involved in the FBI hostilities and threats against me. And as events went, Susan did become visibly, disturbingly, and ominously involved in the FBI hostilities and threats against me — in an manifest way demonstrating that the August 2015 Pequot Library gang-stalking/social cleansing incident was not only alarming in itself, but was the genesis of and blueprint for FBI activity that would reach beyond the grounds of the Pequot Library to become woven into all aspects of my life.

Although details of how Susan was drawn in to the FBI's targeting program cannot be known, conception of them is possible. Susan undoubtedly knew that varied members of Pequot Library staff and book-sale volunteers had been enlisted by the FBI. In most cases, these staff members and volunteers would have been recruited readily. I have no idea what the FBI could have said about me to dispose these individuals to take part in the FBI's demented program. But considering that the FBI signaled its targeting of me by communicating to me that I was seen by the bureau as tantamount to Taliban in an incident about 2012 in the Fairfield Public Library, the FBI could have said anything about me. The FBI's perversity and malevolence is such that it has no qualms about defaming and demonizing someone while representing itself as combatting crime and acting patriotically.

It's not hard to see how many and even most individuals would be amenable to taking a part in an FBI targeting program, especially when taking part was simple, convenient, and entailed no risk. What individuals do not realize though is that in accordance with the FBI's perversity and malevolence, this initial approach is the first step in involving them in the FBI's perversity and malevolence and virtually consigning them to be part of the FBI cult. Once an FBI stooge, always an FBI stooge. As with any demented, deviant cult of any sort, getting out of the cult of the FBI once one has committed oneself to it, however slightly, is extremely difficult and often life-threatening. So sure of its powers of falsification and intimidation is the FBI, it operates as if it considers that virtually everyone can be enlisted into its cult.

Susan Ei knew that despite whatever her own thoughts were about FBI activity at the Pequot Library, she was inevitably in an environment formed by the FBI. Resignation may have been the primary pathway by which Susan entered the atmosphere of hostility toward me and developing plans for a vicious targeting incident that was somewhat complex and involved multiple players, not only FBI agents but library employees as well to be executed at an appropriate time. The planned targeting incident would have been like a project which several staff members were to be a part of, and which other staff members and probably also book-sale volunteers and even some board members knew about.

There would have been buzz about the targeting incident as staff members reaffirmed among themselves that they were still committed to be a part of and that the incident was still on although its exact time was not known. Staff members slated to participate would have been always primed to go into action when an appropriate moment arrived. As it happened, the moment arrived about midday on August 25, 2015, when I was at the library to get some work done at my computer sitting at one of the tables in the main room. A warm day late in August, the library was nearly empty. There were no patrons in the main room where I was. There were more staff than patrons, and enough staff given roles available for the incident to take place. Word from the FBI who had conceived the incident and recruited the library staff, and all was in place, and all unfolded as I made my way to the library, entered, went to the copy machine, and then sat at one of the tables, opened my computer, and began my work for the day.

As we see, the bizarre, yet ominous FBI August 25 targeting incident was not the culmination of the FBI's perversity and malevolence, but rather a phase of it and also a marking of an escalation. Within a couple of days of the incident, Pequot Library custodian appeared at the Fairfield Public Library at a time when I was there, making sure that I caught sight of him, while avoiding any recognition of me such as a nod or look at me, passing animatedly and quickly through my field of view like an automaton across a screen. The FBI would build exponentially on this extension of the August 2015 incident at the Library with its similar recruitment and programming of Susan Ei, who exhibited the same overt movements to guarantee to catch my attention along with the same absence of any related admission that this was what she had done when she succeeded in this. Catching my attention was the aim, with this sufficing to affirm that I was aware of the particular targeting incident, and it was therefore a success.

Susan was targeted especially by the FBI for its extension of the hostility reflected in the August 2015 incident because of her resistance to participation in the August incident. Perhaps Susan had agreed to participate in the incident, Maybe in sitting at her desk in the library children's section in clear sight by me when I would be at the copying machine to run off the N. Y. Times' crossword puzzle, Susan was stationing herself so that I would know that she too, like other employees who had more active roles in the plan, was communicating to me that the FBI had gotten her to be a member of its targeting program.

Since I did not see Susan looking toward me when I was at the computer, nor did she make any indication she was even aware that I was operating the copying machine a few yards off in the direction she was facing, nor register any mutual notice between us as I looked toward her briefly simply recognizing the presence of another person as normal during a pause in the copying of the crossword puzzle, if what I was seeing was Susan's participation in the gang-stalking/social cleansing incident, it didn't register to me as such. It was too benign, too familiar, too normal. Susan seemed focused on some task. I didn't pay much attention, since the scene was so familiar. I simply noticed she was at her desk.

Despite appearances, there's no doubt Susan knew of the malicious FBI plan to target me one day at the Pequot Library, better a day sooner rather than later for the FBI. Whatever her degree of knowledge of the planned targeting incident and decision of how she would relate to it, she showed no indication to me that she was a willing participant. Although Susan would have been dismayed or at least disappointed in knowing that other employees had agreed to cooperate in the FBI targeting plan, she was too close to them and too loyal to the library to alert me or make objections to any higher-up or board member. She wouldn't be going along in any significant way, but she wouldn't interfere either.

When I filed my civil case against the library and certain employees, and Susan Ei was not named as a defendant, the FBI could only conclude that Susan either had not played a role in the targeting incident to the FBI's satisfaction or that her behavior was not seen by me to communicate to me that she had any part in the scheme. Like executive director Montilla approaching me at the July 2015 library book fair, Susan Ei sitting normally, inoffensively, ostensibly at her desk unaware that the scheme was unfolding right before her when I was at the copying machine marked her as an employee to now become programmed to be a visible, unmistakeable, and with Susan, a repeated part of the FBI's targeting. In the FBI's eyes, Susan had to become involved to demonstrate not only to me, but also to everyone at the Pequot Library the FBI's ability to influence others to further the FBI's designs.

By declining to manifestly be a part of the FBI August 25, 2015, Pequot Library disturbing FBI targeting incident of me or perhaps in failing to play the part assigned to her so I would see that she too had been enlisted by the FBI, and thus not appearing as a defendant in my lawsuit against the library, Susan Ei made herself a target of the FBI. By demonstrating her independence and repugnance over the FBI scheme involving Pequot Library employees, Susan Ei was challenging the FBI's pathological assumption that its intents and operations outweigh and override an individual's notions of her independence; and Susan's repugnance toward the FBI inherent in Susan's exercise of independence by not being a part of the plan of the August 2015 targeting incident offended the FBI, which in its megalomania — another aspect of its pathology— sees itself as beyond criticism. The FBI August 2015 gang-stalking/social cleansing involving Pequot Library employees also went against everything the Library held itself out as representing with respect to being a welcoming place where patrons could read, study, and work in an peaceful setting, employing individuals who had patrons' interests in mind, and other values instilled in libraries.

As for the FBI, it felt betrayed by Susan in that she had not overtly participated in the demented August 25 gang-stalking/social cleansing incident. Susan would have to pay for this.

10. "Suggestion of Death"

Unlike Pequot Library employees Adair Heitmann, Denise Martin, and Robert Repko, Susan Ei took her position and her work at the Pequot Library seriously. In appointing her as children's librarian, the library was evidencing to her, patrons, and the broader community that she was one to be trusted to represent and fulfill the library's ideals, values, and purposes. Susan Ei took this appointment seriously, as the Library knew she would.

While Susan Ei's sense of professionalism and personal moral code put her in the position of at most reluctantly being a part of the August 2015 targeting incident so that if she was being involved at all, she sat at her desk that day in such a demeanor and distance that her involvement was unnoticeable to me, there was a simple reason and a simple motive why she demurred from materially participating in the FBI scheme. This reason and related motivation is that Susan Ei regarded herself as genuinely and absolutely interested in and concerned about the welfare and lives of children, and particularly children who made use of the children's department of the Pequot Library that Susan was the head of with the title children's librarian. For Susan by her personality, general moral outlook, work with younger persons throughout much of her life, position at the Pequot Library she sought, values and responsibilities of her position as children's librarian, and her example, education, desires and hopes for children she worked with directly and for all children, and beliefs about what makes for a desirable and acceptable society, involvement in a malicious scheme with elements of criminality that the FBI was preparing for at the Pequot Library and enlisting library staff members to be a part of was an anathema.

Susan Ei — similar to myself— with her higher education, good nature, humaneness, sense of personal responsibility, and social conscience was problematic for the FBI. The FBI would have to use especially energetic, persistent, and variously overtly and implicitly threatening techniques to change her into what it aimed for to conduce to its malevolent schemes. Unlike Susan Ei who saw and took her position as children's librarian as a reflection of her true and best self and enjoyed the image of the Pequot Library as a distinctive library with a venerable heritage located in a prime section of the town of Fairfield, namely Southport, Pequot Library employees Adair Heitman, Denise Martin, and Robert Repko saw their association with Pequot Library as little more than talking points hopefully indicating to others that they shared at least some of the repute and status of the library. Where Susan Ei represented the values, desired image, and aspirations of the library, Adair Heitman, Denise Martin, and Robert Repko were like hanger-ons who enjoyed trafficking in the reputation and image of the Pequot Library for whatever benefit this had on their interest in their own image and presumed elevation in status.

Susan Ei knew that prestige was attached to the position of children's librarian at the Pequot Library. But this was not what was most important to her as it is for the majority of the Pequot Library employees. Susan Ei wanted the position of children's librarian because it gave her the opportunity to do the most good with her life, talents, and desires as she understood and likely realized she would be able to accomplish in her life. Given the position, she dedicated herself to it. FBI intimidations, inducements, and pressures were affronts and assailments to this dedication, Susan's commitments were basics of her identity and her identification that aligned with the institutional purpose and responsibilities of the Pequot Library, as she realized in seeking and accepting the position of children's librarian. Children's librarian of the Pequot Library was thus an ideal occupation for Susan Ei, or close to it.

Whereas Adair Heitman, Denise Martin, Robert Repko, book-sale volunteers and other Pequot Library employees and volunteers who in various ways played a part in the FBI targeting of me at the library were easily brought into the FBI's schemes because their attachment to the library was superficial, self-serving, and essentially selfish, given Susan Ei's dedication, knowledge that she was accomplishing good, and knowing that she was contributing to the tradition, reputation, image, and purpose of the Pequot Library, the most Susan Ei could hope for in lending herself in any way to the FBI influence overtaking the library and the FBI's plans for me was that she would be conflicted, split.

For an honest, open, self-respecting individual with integrity such as Susan Ei, presenting herself one way, in Susan's case mainly as a capable and in some ways exceptional children's librarian, while seeing, being immersed in, and in some way being a part of the FBI's plans if only by association inevitably creates inner conflict, and this is continually disturbing. Such a situation creates a feeling of a false self, of having to act rather than to behave spontaneously, of being calculating in many situations lest a careless, revealing word slip out, of suspicions that others in on the scheme are always judging one for one's loyalty to the group and to the scheme. Such a situation as Susan knew herself to be in whatever form this took also implants suspicions of others that they might be in on the scheme and spying on one in one's interactions with them to report to the FBI agents who had designed the scheme and who were active in the library to make sure that their scheme would play out as planned.

With such a situation come feelings of hyperawareness and repression. One fears making a mistake to the point that this becomes an obsession. Although a mistake in saying something in a conversation or perhaps letting something secret slip out to one's spouse or partner may be innocent, ones such as FBI agents desiring, expecting, and commanding commitment and silence about what they had devised would take this at least as indicating to them that they had made a mistake in counting on the individual. But no matter that a mistake revealing the plot was innocent, the FBI would see only that their plotting had been compromised, and they would feel vulnerable and betrayed, There would be consequences — perhaps to a spouse, perhaps to a spouse's business, perhaps to a child's education at a university, perhaps to one's own position, such as children's librarian.

The twin feelings of hyperawareness and repression were like a chemical reaction bubbling away in Susan's personality, corroding her firm, developed sense of self at about age 60, continually exciting her consciousness in unbidden, new ways, casting up doubts about the outer and inner worlds so that each was distorted as in a wavy fun house mirror. Former references for identity and behavior attenuated, mere coping became primary, each day and each instance of coping a blow to Susan's self-esteem, self-confidence, self-sufficiency, sense of resourcefulness, and independence. Susan's sense of self was being supplanted, taken over by the FBI's pathology enforced by intimidations, blandishments, and unnerving manifest presence and interactions with other library employees which now entailed communal knowledge of the FBI's influences and were unsettling as well despite being comparatively subtle. The tone and configurations of the environment had changed.

The hyperawareness coming from being targeted by the FBI for at least awareness of or more likely to some degree participation in their malicious scheme made Susan's surroundings seem almost liked they glowed, like they were almost lurid, as if reaching into her to evoke memories, perceptions, feelings, thoughts as they never had before. It was as the surroundings conspired in the FBI's scheme, all part of the trap the FBI was laying out, all part of the scenario as if the FBI had come to possess them and they were no longer normal, relevant, useful elements of Susan's daily life in her activities with children and work space shared with other staff. Nothing was the same at the Pequot Library.

For the staff such as Adair Heitman, Denise Martin, and Robert Repko, the hyperawareness was stimulation. It made them feel more alive, as FBI attention of targeting them made them feel more important. They were no longer lower-end, incidental employees of Pequot Library filling routine jobs. Targeted by the FBI and told the FBI was counting on them for the success of the mission presented as worthy, these other staff were imbued with a sense of purpose, enlivened by anticipation of when the gang-stalking/social cleansing incident would take place, felt strengthened by membership in the group of participants, and felt rewarded by the new dimension that had been added to their relationships with one another thanks to the FBI with its cultish principles, techniques, values, and goals. Heitman, Martin, and Repko felt grateful to the FBI.

By contrast, Susan had no need for nor secret, latent desire to have herself seem to be augmented by succumbing to FBI targeting. Her position and activities as children's librarian gave her purpose and offered fulfillment. Also, in her position, she had responsibilities to the library, to its patrons and their children, and to the public which were like a shield to ward off FBI appeals and persuasion. Nonetheless, in the circumstances saturated by FBI influence and intentions in which other staff were contributing to and even the property of the Pequot Library was to be used for the eventual gang-stalking/social cleansing incident, Susan was made vulnerable. With her strong sense of identification with the Pequot Library, now that the majority of the staff were identifying with the presence and plans of the FBI, Susan became disposed to join in, though with reservations and provisions according to her knowledge of her independence, intelligence, and commitments.

When first lending herself in a limited way to the FBI plans involving the Pequot Library location and certain staff, Susan probably never knew that later she would be the one the FBI chose to stalk me after I filed my lawsuit against the library and staff I identified as taking part in the August 2015 gang-stalking/social cleansing targeting incident. Susan felt she had done her part, and would be left alone once the planned targeting incident had taken place toward the end of August 2015 and as happened, I was barred from the Pequot Library upon informing the executive director and higher staff including Susan of what was behind the targeting, namely the FBI originally targeting me out of its associations with Democratic Party figures and operatives in Connecticut and state's attorneys. Since I was no longer allowed at the library under threat of arrest for trespass, how to relate to me or participation in a vicious targeting incident would no longer be an issue for Susan.

Robert Repko's appearance at the Fairfield Public Library a couple of days or so after the August 25, 2015, incident at the Pequot Library was the FBI's sign to me that it intended that its reach extend beyond the Pequot Library and it had the power to turn individuals I had known for decades into instruments of disturbance and menace against me. Having been targeted for so long and in such a variety of ways, including ways involving individuals I had known for a long time and been friendly with, and often by persons I didn't know in approaching me in the interest of making my acquaintance, I was aware of the FBI's reach and delight in undermining personal and also business relationships of mine by lies about me and intimidation of various individuals. Nonetheless, the FBI, out of compulsiveness and perversity, persisted in replaying such messages to me over and over as part of its program for remolding (warping) reality for an individual and a community.

While Susan Ei couldn't have known a lot about the FBI's multifaceted targeting program of me which had become a part of the FBI's operations and strange agenda throughout Fairfield County and neighboring areas of Connecticut including New York City as I recognized in occasional trips there, as a Pequot Library employee, she did come to know that the FBI was determined to target me, and she did come to know about the FBI's measures such as defamation and intimidation to bring individuals into its targeting plans directly by the FBI's approaches to her and indirectly by seeing the FBI's approaches to other staff. Yet, for all Susan had come to know and the ways she had seen she had changed by the FBI's interactions with her and the ways she was seeing that other staff members and the Pequot Library as an institution had changed by the FBI's widespread, systematic activity at the library, she never imagined that she would be put to the activity of stalking on multiple occasions eventually to the point of giving up to the FBI her distinctive, dark metallic green Honda SUV making her in effect an essential part of the FBI's malevolence carried to within yards of where I lived by being visibly parked outside my apartment. Susan Ei's minimal, fleeting, and anodyne presence during the unfolding of the FBI's alarming August 2015 targeting incident of me at the Pequot Library by sitting at her desk in the children's department where I could not miss seeing her when I was at the copying machine and where I had seen her countless times before was probably for Susan the limit of what she believed the FBI would require of her — if she was in fact an incidental part of the targeting incident more by knowing it was unfolding than willing, active participant such as employees Adair Heitmann and Denise Martin — and also the limit and the manner of any willingness she gave to be a part, namely, simply presence as sign of support while demurring with respect to particular behavior regarding the steps and mechanics of the unfolding of the incident.

Because Susan did not and probably because of her pleasant nature and knowledge she was doing good in her life could not imagine what would be in store for her when the FBI felt threatened by exposure of their malevolence at the venerable, prized institution of the Pequot Library, the FBI's approach to her to stalk me as a means of intimidation and forewarning of more worrisome actions should I pursue my lawsuit would have been an especially cruel and heedless tack. That the FBI not only felt threatened itself, but also saw the threat to the library staff named as defendants in my case and the library itself as an organization with liability gave the FBI's efforts to coerce Susan heightened force and urgency. It was not that the FBI felt responsibility for the library and the employees being sued, for if it had a sense of responsibility, the FBI would not have infiltrated the library in the first place.

The FBI was concerned about its own image and reputation — more a media-supported myth than reality — for professionalism and effectiveness. That the FBI is rarely mentioned in the media or portrayed in entertainment shows without also commenting on its "special agents" and status as the "premier law-enforcement agency" is testimony to how the myth of the FBI created by the FBI's public-relations operation with the cooperation of sympathetic media and politicians has been implanted in the public. For the FBI to be seen not only as having targeted the Pequot Library and members of its staff to be a part of its operations — which were silly and infantile besides being malicious and threatening, and had no justification — but also as not having dictatorial control over the situation the FBI had created despite the secrecy and coercive power going into its creation exposed fault lines running through the FBI as an organization making laughable its claim as the "premier law-enforcement agency" while also exposing its shaky foundation and the folly and recklessness its so-called "special agents" were given to.

The objects of the FBI's targeting being exposed by me in my lawsuit, social media postings, and emails to journalists, public officials, and others were also grounds for ridicule of the FBI. Librarians?! Library workers?! A children's librarian at the Pequot Library?! These were not the junkies, prostitutes, derelicts, rummies, individuals compromised by crimes, foreigners of questionable U. S. residency, and such the FBI typically strong-armed for roles in its operations. Moreover, the FBI's operation was in itself unjustifiable, self-evidently vindictive, and malicious and treacherous to boot. The FBI scheme was not only malicious and treacherous toward me, but toward the Pequot Library individuals the FBI approached to be involved. They were for the most suburban individuals living in one of the country's most desirable areas, married with children, a number successful, some to the point of being wealthy. Their involvement was scandalous, as they knew and the FBI knew. There was great pressure on all involved to cover-up what was going on; hence the viciousness, widening, and escalation of the targeting of me following the August 2015 incident not only exposing the FBI's infiltration of the library, but the knowledge of this and cooperation in it by most of the Pequot Library staff and the board of directors upon my email to the executive director and others about the alarming targeting incident.

All of this — the fact of the gang-stalking/social cleansing incident, the susceptibility of the Pequot Library employees to lend themselves to the FBI scheme, the continuing presence of the FBI at the library to work to cover-up aspects of the scheme they could, my lawsuit naming the library and employees as defendants, staff and board members nervousness and concerns that they would be named as my lawsuit and investigation progressed with the shame and liability going with this, the expectations of staff that Susan would come to their aid as the FBI — which knew all about intimidation of a target and cover-up of its crimes and the crimes of its accomplices — saw fit, the distress of the FBI in having its venality and treacherousness exposed, the FBI's determination to engage in greater degrees of intimidation of me, the FBI's movement to widen the group of individuals involved in the targeting of, thus marginalizing me more — swept into Susan like a turgid tide.

Susan's status and reputation which she had earned over years and which her prominent position as children's librarian at the Pequot Library was both the ultimate confirmation of and welcome, valued reward for in her own eyes were to now be used by the FBI to try to put greater pressure on me, and so in fact be used against Susan — almost as if the prized position of her life was being held against her — in that the FBI showed no respect for this, but crudely and cruelly weaponized Susan and her achievements. Susan's highest achievement in her life, the one she was proudest of and saw as the means to accomplish the most good as she defined this, was in effect being used against her by the FBI as it was concomitantly being used against me. The FBI apparently expected that because of the high regard of Susan at the library and members of the community who knew her and her demonstrably admirable and respected character in being entrusted to be a model for and to work with children at the Library, I would see the error of my ways and recognize the virtues of the FBI. For the FBI, the aura of Susan was supposed to overshadow the FBI's crimes and corruption I knew about and was experiencing continually. The reasoning and even the thought that this would be so is warped and desperate, I know. But this is the way the FBI thinks.

The FBI thinking had no effect on my understanding of and judgment about what was going on, namely widespread, metastasizing FBI crime and corruption causing varied harms not only in my life, but also the lives of many others and to the social system. The FBI enterprise of having Susan stalk me including placement of her Honda SUV close to my apartment was a waste of Susan's persona and time at her expense with respect to bring about any change in my perspective and investigative and reporting activities. The warped and desperate thinking of the FBI going into the enterprise of having Susan stalk me at places away from the Pequot Library only to have her actions wasted was like a black hole of nihilism. It was warped and futile, a hole out of which nothing good could come.

My respect for Susan was such that I felt sorry for her. Knowing that she was an exceptional person, I intuitively understood the exceptional pressures the FBI would have had to place her under to get her to engage in such obviously criminal actions that went against her nature and mores. While I felt sorry for her, I had no idea of the turmoil she must have been experiencing inwardly, and I doubt anyone else did. Undoubtedly the FBI gave her assurances or implied that because of its prowess and reputation which could spread fear in a community and quell any opposition, she should have no concerns about adverse effects from engaging in the stalking. Oafish, obtuse, and self-centered to the point of exclusion of any other concern, the FBI would not have any concerns about adverse effects for Susan. It's not that the FBI would have thought about such and ruled them out or minimized them to the point of being highly improbable. It's that with the FBI — oafish, obtuse, self-centered to the point of exclusion of any other concern — such concerns would not have come to mind. And while Susan's fellow and sister employees would naturally have such concerns as would come to most normal persons, they would not raise them with Susan nor with the FBI as objections to its plans for Susan; for the FBI's plans for Susan were seen as an effort to contribute to the cover-up of their unseemly involvement with the FBI and defend them from damage to their respective images and from accountability and liability.

Fully mature, always friendly (more than poised), with a network of fellow and sister employees and friends, married with two daughters, engaged in many activities including creation of activities and art work for children, gardening, and book collecting, Susan could have never conceived she would be in such a situation, a black hole from which there was no way out. She had been surrounded by a network of persons and range of activities which had been nourishing for her, and to which she gave nourishment. For her this was not simply the stereotypical "support network," but was the many dimensions of her life, giving it richness, color, volume, depth. Where was it now, this support network? FBI and library employees were depending on her to play her part, the part devised by the FBI under the exigency of desperately trying to save its own reputation and image of professionalism and competence, a part requiring a greater degree of participation, visibility, and commitment than with any other staff member — this part extending far beyond the location of the library, adding new dimensions to the targeting of me, now for Susan, who at most on the day of the gang-stalking/social cleansing incident at the library had sat at her desk appearing to go about her business as normal.

Susan could not have told friends about her compromising agreement with the FBI to engage in stalking of a long-time patron of the Library. It's doubtful she told her husband, who probably would have discouraged her from getting so involved with the FBI, and may even have gone to higher-ups in the FBI, state politicians, influential people in Southport, or the media to try to prevent what was being done to his wife. It's improbable Susan said anything to her daughters. It's not that Susan would have been lying, or trying to cover up anything. For there was nothing to lie about, nothing to cover up — not in the time before my amended complaint in my lawsuit against her with details of my claims describing her actions was filed. Susan would have been uneasy internally. But she would not have had to face, to explain, to justify, to rationalize, to answer entreaties and questions about her actions. Explaining, justifying, rationalizing, answering to relatives and friends of her network would have been wrenching for Susan and for them.

The relationships would never have been the same. Puzzles about Susan, suspicions, questions about her stability, who she was, who she saw herself to be would be inevitable among some. Even those who offered support and understanding, an element of any support network, would be offering support and understanding for something that was strange. Given Susan's high standards for herself and her acceptance that she was a role model for children and daughters, she would have known that support and understanding was not merited nor deserved. She would have felt saddened that the well-meaning friends and relatives would have been disposed to offer support and understanding. She never wanted to do anything like this to them. She never wanted to have something like this done to her.

The FBI and Pequot Library individuals invested more in Susan than she could bear. Upon the filing of the public document of my amended complaint, Susan underwent the trauma of exposure; which trauma before long lapsed into despair. Despair was magnified and complicated by the feeling of loneliness. Though Susan still had her circle of friends, the library staff, her husband, her family, the questions which had inevitably been generated about her even by ones professing understanding of her actions and offering the most support had changed the essence of her relationships with all. Although the questions may not have been openly asked, all, Susan and the others, knew they were there, like laundry rippling in the breeze, silent, animate, ghostly.

9. "This is Getting Really Serious"

On March 23, 2017, when I was in the clerk's office at the Bridgeport Superior
Court on Main Street waiting in line to file a document in my lawsuit against the
Fairfield Public Library for defamation, false statements to police, and other
claims similar to my claims against the Pequot Library and defendants in that
case, there was a young woman standing at the left end of the counter. As I — and
anyone else in line — could not help seeing and overhearing, this young woman
was talking loudly to one of the clerks sitting at a desk abut 6 feet away from the
counter seemingly trying to find information to help the young woman with
whatever the issue was. The young woman was urging the clerk she was speaking
loudly toward, but not concertedly to, "This is getting really serious." Several
times she let the clerk know in different words that the matter was "serious."
Besides her words that the matter was "serious," the young woman evidenced this
by her stressed body language — pushing her head forward as she was speaking
loudly to the clerk, moving agitatedly in place, and glancing around at me and
others in the clerk's office with an expression of mixed apology and explanation.

As a clerk came to one of the counter windows where one drops off documents for
filing, as I approached to drop off my document, my attention turned from the
woman speaking loudly about a "serious" matter. In the few seconds it took me to
get to the counter and begin to tell the clerk what my document was, In the
moment it took for me to present my document for filing telling the clerk what it
was, the situation of the woman telling the clerk still sitting a a desk loudly
enough so that everyone standing in line in the clerk's office could hear that the
matter was "serious.", the situation had ended.

The "serious" matter had ended abruptly, apparently pressing of it at the clerk's
office by level of voice and body movements in such a way to be sure to make the
impression that it was "serious" timed to coincide with my presence in the clerk's
office.

When I left the clerk's office and walked out of the Superior Court by the back
door to the plaza behind the building, the young woman who had been talking
loudly and agitatedly to the clerk in the clerk's office was standing about 15 yards
from the back door (the only one open so one can exit from it) along the path I

would take to get from the exit and where my car was parked. I would have to pass right by her.

The woman I had seen in the clerk's office was facing sideways slightly turned toward me with her face toward me as if she was wanting to have something to say. Indeed, I assumed she was since she remained in the same spot I would have to walk by, looking at me from the time I had walked a few paces out the back door, and presuming she had seen me in the clerk's office less than a minute earlier since she had looked right at me a few times. Looking at her, I slowed as I got close to her to show that I was ready to listen to what she had to say.

As I got to about four feet from the woman looking at her and just as I stopped, abruptly from my right approached a young African-American woman. I noticed her out of the corner of my right eye. She was relatively tall, on the thin side, and nice looking. I was startled since I hadn't noticed her with my attention since leaving the court from the back door on the young woman I had seen in the clerk's office.

The movement of the African-American woman moving toward me caused me to turn my head in her direction. She continued to approach me obviously meaning to get my attention and have some interaction with me. I watched her for a second mainly to be assured she would not walk into me she seemed so intent on distracting me.

Stopped now and somewhat confused and torn between what to be paying attention to, I turned my face to again look at the young woman from the clerk's office who had by every indication wanted to say something to me. But she had turned and was walking away, back to me. So I looked again at the African-American woman. But she now had turned, and was walking away. I continued to my car.

I chalked this incident up as one more such incident of FBI agents or accomplices targeting me. At first I did not know what to make of it except that it was yet one more strange incident that was a part of the FBI's targeting of me by agents or proxies composed of irrational, odd elements apparently meant to at least disconcert me, but also with the larger aim of upsetting my daily activities and pushing me along the path to insanity or outbursts of violence, thereby "proving" the FBI's claim that I was insane and/or violent. Especially, the element of the incident that the matter was getting serious which I had heard the woman say loudly in the clerk's office was puzzling. I presumed I was being informed that one or more of my lawsuits was moving or had moved to a point where it was being taken more seriously by defendants. I had no idea why they would be thinking this since while the claims of my lawsuits were serious in that they inferred menacing, physical threats, and other intentional hostile acts toward me to me with possible costly liabilities, the claims had been stated at the outset of my lawsuits, and anything that was going on at the time was routine in a lawsuit.

I happened to see Susan Ei one last time. Or maybe I didn't just happen to — maybe it was yet another staged incident.

At some time between the Monday, March 20, 2017, and the Friday, March 24, after I had checked mail at my post office box at the Southport Post office, I came face-to-face with Susan on Pequot Road. Facing east, I was stopped at the stop sign at the intersection of Pequot Avenue and Old Post Road, the Spic and Span Market to my right. Facing me in her car going west on Pequot Avenue was Susan in her distinctive metallic green Honda SUV. I recognized her clearly in looking at her as she looked at me for a few seconds as usual at an intersection with stop signs for all directions to watch which direction a vehicle encountered was going so as to proceed cautiously and safely. I looked at her more glancingly than with recognition. as if she were any other driver facing me in such a driving situation. She looked at me the same. And we drove on in our separate directions.

11. "Suggestion of Death"

On April 3, 2017, I received a "Suggestion of Death" notice from Susan Ei's defense attorney, Brian Paice of the Hartford area law firm Conway Stoughton, in the lawsuit which had been assigned to judge Michael Kamp at the Bridgeport Superior Court.

Paice and Kamp had themselves been involved in FBI witness intimidation and threats against me, in their cases by gratuitously and showily sporting medical braces intended to impress on me the FBI's targeting of me and threats of death or physical injury. Lawyer Paice's and judge Kamp's medical braces were elements of the FBI's practice of "semiotics of terrorism." As the FBI knew from monitoring my iPhone and emails, a little while before, I had been told about a serious, potentially life-threatening injury sustained by a relative requiring constant medical attention. In accordance with the logic of the FBI's semiotics of terrorism, they knew signs of medical troubles would call to my mind the state and vulnerability of my relative, which would naturally stir in me my own awareness of the state of being targeted the FBI had formed about me and as a central part of this, my own concerns about the death threats and possibility of incapacitating physical injury.

Lawyer Paice sported his medical brace on one of his ankles. In one instance this was complemented by crutches, Paice hobbling into the courtroom two hours after the hearing had been scheduled to start making a pitiful spectacle of himself as everyone knowledgeable about what was going on recognized. The judge Kamp demonstrated a particular flair in sporting his gratuitous medical brace. On the day of one hearing in the Bridgeport Superior Court, Kamp, who knew by then that he had been appointed as the judge for my case against Susan Ei, while I and Paice with his medical brace were standing at the counter in the courthouse's sixth-floor case-flow office, Kamp suddenly wheeled in behind me off my right shoulder making such a commotion and coming so close to me that I turned around to see what was going on. There was the judge, brandishing his medical brace on a forearm. Despite his flourish, Judge Kamp wasn't acting. As new judge, he was genuinely thrilled and proud the FBI had chosen him to be a conspicuous player in its program of targeting me. As judge Kamp realized, it is not everyone who is called to be chosen by the FBI for delivering death threats to particularly nettlesome targets. For Kamp, being selected to be an FBI stooge was testament that he had arrived.

"Suggestion of death" is an odd legal term for a court filing giving notice to all parties and to the public that an individual who was a party in the lawsuit has died. The wikipedia entry on it is, "A suggestion of death, in law, refers to calling the death of a party to the attention of a court and making it a matter of record, as a step in the revival of an action abated by the death of a party." There was no "suggestion" about it though. Susan Ei was dead.

Attorney Paice's filing of the required "suggestion of death" notice was the first I learned that Susan Ei had died, on March 31, 2017 as the document stated. Simultaneously upon learning this fact, the thought that the FBI had been somehow involved in her death came to mind. The timing between the ruling by the District Federal Court that my case against Susan Ei be remanded to the Bridgeport Superior Court recorded on the PACER log of the Federal Court on March 9, my amended complaint detailing the stalking incidents and the ones with Susan's green Honda SUV parked by my apartment filed on March 16, the logging in of the Federal Court's remand order on the Connecticut judicial website's log of the case (FBT-CV16-5032337-S) on March 29, and Susan's death on March 31 was too obviously interconnected to be coincidence. And indeed, the series of events was also demonstrably logically progressive. Especially with the FBI's recklessness, cynical use of Susan, and adverse effects of the FBI's activities on some individuals and organizations as I was seeing, that grave misfortune had befallen Susan Ei came naturally and immediately to mind.

Intertwined with my thought that the FBI use of Susan Ei in its targeting of me had led to her sudden, untimely death was my memory of the ambiguous, puzzling incident at the Bridgeport Superior Court clerk's office in mid-March 2017 when I was there to file some papers where the younger woman standing at the counter had been speaking loudly across a space of some six feet in the direction of a clerk sitting at a desk who was not engaged in any way with her beyond being aware that there was this woman standing at the counter speaking loudly. The woman at the counter was saying over and over, three or more times, "This is getting serious," seemingly imploring the clerk to do something about whatever was getting serious as quickly as possible. By the time of this incident happening only a couple of weeks earlier than I got the notice of Susan's death, I had come to recognize the often silly, but apparently supposedly portentous or meaningful behavior of the FBI in its targeting. I knew from the loud way the young woman at the counter was repeating that something was "getting serious," her occasional glances in my direction, and the clerk's absence of any sense of urgency indicating she understood that she was simply prop in the staged incident that the scene has been devised to communicate something to me.

The young woman speaking loudly left the clerk's office a moment before I approached the counter when a clerk was free to leave the legal document I had come to file. But as I found, this was not the end of this staged incident. As I walked across the plaza at the back of the courthouse in leaving, I again encountered the woman who had been speaking loudly, this time positioned where I could not miss seeing her. She seemed to have been waiting outside for me to come out. I wondered if she wanted to say something directly to me. But as I got within a couple of yards of her, she abruptly walked off, to me emphasizing that the incident was over. While I had been unable to discern any particular "message" in this incident, the note that something was "serious" lingered with me.

Considering the death threats I had gotten and frequent menacing incidents at the post office, grocery stores, wine shops, and other places in my errands, my first thought was that something serious, something more serious was going to happen or start happening to me. As I continued with my postings about the targeting of me and related matters of public interest, which were often exposures of crime and corruption and sometimes named particular individuals, at different times there were escalations of the targeting with concomitant increased dangers to me. The August 2015 gang-stalking/social cleansing incident at the Pequot Library involving multiple staff members and FBI agents working concertedly was one such escalation.

Being informed by the incident at the clerk's office that there was something "serious" afoot, I had been on the lookout for what this would be. I was even more wary. This was the state I was in when I received notice that the "suggestion of death" court document had been filed.

Although it did not occur to me that Susan would suffer grave consequences in knowingly participating in the FBI's targeting program of me since while I saw what I presumed were adverse consequences on some individuals such as leaving a position someone had at a library, I had seen nothing that I would call "serious." Susan knew what she was doing, and she knew that I had filed lawsuits against other staff at the library who had engaged in hostile, threatening, egregious actions against me. Nonetheless, in an instant upon hearing she had died, I knew that something tragic, but also predictable had happened. I wasn't surprised. I guess I knew it was only a matter of time before the FBI's activities in the area went from extreme and perverse to deadly.

There was more however in giving definition to my awareness that the FBI targeting of Susan Ei had been responsible for her death.

11. The Aftermath of Susan Ei's Death

I first heard about the Bridgeport lawyer Peter Tsimbidaros from mention of him in news articles about two men who had been convicted of a 1993 murder in New Haven and had served 16 years in prison. Tsimbidaros had succeeded in getting their convictions overturned primarily on the basis of recanted testimony by key prosecution witness who was a drug addict who had been interrogated by police for over six hours. The Connecticut Supreme Court later overruled the judge's ruling that "actual innocence" of the two had been proven, and ordered the men returned to prison.

Peter was in photos in news articles and in television clips. I saw him a few times when we were in the Bridgeport Superior Court at the same time for hearings. He lived in Black Rock less than a mile from me. At some time, like other Black Rock residents, he began using the Fairfield Public Library, presumably like me and the others, for its facilities which were better and accessibility which was easier from Black Rock, which borders Fairfield, than the Bridgeport Public Library. Black Rock has a branch of the Bridgeport Library system, but it has limited space and facilities.

When I'd see Peter at the Fairfield Public Library, he was usually sitting at one of the long desks in the magazine room. He would work on legal briefs and do research. Coming to the Library, I would know he was there by seeing his dark gray Honda CR-V parked in the library parking lot. A couple of times I had seen him removing loads of paperwork from it, and going into the library.

Although we never interacted at the library, Peter knew I was pursuing cases about serious matters at the Bridgeport Superior Court and also posting provocative and often accusatory articles on social media. I knew Peter would know this. All the local lawyers knew me as the individual who was engaged in the lawsuits and social postings. The matters of legal ethics, criminal acts and corruption, associations and networks of individuals and organizations, and image of the legal profession were not ones lawyers would ignore. As well, I was engaged with scandalous matters, and lawyers are drawn to follow scandals as much as others.

I had called Peter Tsimbidaros in September 2015 following the August targeting incident of me at the Pequot Library after I had done some legal research on menacing, trespass, and other matters entailed in the situation which had developed. I called him three times, and left messages on his answering machine. As I told him, I wanted to consult with him about my situation, particularly how to deal with the no-trespass order against me with notice that I would be arrested for trespass if I "set foot" on the property of the library. As I told him, I would pay him what he would charge for an hour's consultation. Although I didn't mention a figure, at the time, I had some money to afford this, I was prepared to pay up to $300.00 for consultation.

After my first phone call leaving my message, I never saw Peter Tsimbidaros at the Fairfield Public Library again. I would have spoken to him briefly to see if he had gotten my message and if he was interested in consulting with me if I had. So I called him the second and third time leaving the same message, the third time adding that this would be my last call. In each of the three phone messages, I left my number.

Peter Tsimbidaros knew he could see me at the Fairfield Public Library if he wanted, and he had my number to call if he wanted. And he knew that like him, I was committed to exposing and trying to rectify harmful practices and effects in the legal field. Yet Peter's genuine, ingrained commitment to fair, equal treatment for all and to defense against underhanded and dubious law-enforcement and prosecution schemes to get convictions as he saw from being in the legal field did not keep him from succumbing to FBI intimidations to not have anything to do with me.

There is no other explanation than FBI intimidation to explain Peter's disappearance at the Fairfield Public Library in conjunction with my first phone call to him. It is unusual too for any lawyer not to be open to being contacted about some legal matter relating to the lawyer's respective interests and practice. Most lawyers offer "free consultation" for a first contact with them, during which they decide if they'd be interested in handling a case and proposing to the individual calling that they would take him or her on as a client. In the case of my calling Peter, I didn't assume he would be interested in handling my no-trespass case — which is why I said I would pay him a fee in my messages to him. I knew my case was controversial, and I knew that individuals such as Pequot Library executive director Heather-Marie Montilla and custodian Robert Repko whom the FBI had seen I had a special relationship with were targeted by the FBI with the result that the relationship with them changed radically from good to poor with elements of disfavor and hostility.

Although I knew that the FBI was interfering in my relationships with others by defamation of me and intimidation of others, I thought that conventions and basics of the legal field such as routine lawyer consultations with prospective clients or paid consultations with respect to a lawyer's central interests and expertise would be observed and respected. My right to legal counsel was also in the picture in my contacting Peter Tsimbidaros. For the FBI however, in its demented lawlessness and lust for total population control, legal conventions, professional practices and courtesies, and rights of individuals are trampled on.

As with Susan Ei, with Peter Tsimbidaros, the FBI interfered with my roughly defined, yet mutually acknowledged relationship so that the FBI's perversity, depravity, and hostility came to supplant so as to permanently negate professional standards and practices and social norms. Susan Ei and Peter Tsimbidaros were each targeted by the FBI as surely as I was being targeted, with the effect that the FBI's targeting was multiplied, its grip on the local population spreading and tightening.

I didn't try contacting any other lawyer when it became clear that Peter Tsimbidaros would not be getting in touch with me for a consultation. From what I knew of Peter, he was the lawyer who would be most likely to at least have a consultation with me. Over the years I had tried at times to find a lawyer who would be interested in handling different legal matters which came up. I hadn't been able to find one though. So I gave up trying. I had come to distrust lawyers anyway. I thought that by paying for a one-time consultation with Peter Tsimbidaros, I would get a direct, relevant assessment of my situation while not making him a target of the FBI. This was not to be however.

The FBI's targeting of Peter took my right to legal consultation according to my choice from me as the FBI's targeting of Pequot Library employees had took patronage of the library from me. Driven by perversity and psychopathology as it is, this was not enough for the FBI. The FBI had Susan Ei stalk me at different places away from the Pequot Library, and took control of her Honda SUV to park it multiple times by my apartment about five miles from the Library. And the FBI had lawyer Peter Tsimbidaros end his habit of working at the Fairfield Public Library for his convenience and productivity. The FBI was disrupting not only my life, but the lives of others it was targeting to be a part of the targeting of me.

I had not seen Peter for the last time however. At the time of the death of Susan Ei, he reappeared in my life. The first time I saw him at this time was at the Fairfield Public Library. He had not come to work at a desk in the library magazine room as he had previously though.

I encountered him in the magazine room, but he was not sitting at a desk nor working on anything. Instead, he made sure he caught my attention by standing where I could not miss seeing him along the way I was moving. I noticed him as he intended, and he saw that I did, but I had no response to him.

As was my habit at the library before getting to work I had brought with me, I went to the shelf with the day's New York Times to take out the Arts section to copy the day's crossword puzzle. When I turned from getting the paper to set it on a table to take out the Arts section, Peter was no longer where he had been in the magazine room. I could see he was not anywhere in the magazine room.

Making my way down the ramp leading to the large, sprawling library main room where the copying machine was in a small walled-off area, looking ahead toward the spot where the copying machine was, I saw Peter standing at it. I stopped, and turned around, forgoing my habit of doing the crossword puzzle for the day. I was not interested in walking into an FBI staged incident.Peter was obviously trying to engage with me. I thought it had something to do with the death of Susan Ei. It was no coincidence that he was manifestly making his presence known to me, and standing still looking at me in spots in the library where I would be, plainly wanting to engage with me.

After staying a little longer in the library, not seeing Peter again during this time, I went to the Stop & Shop grocery store on King's Highway Cut-off in Fairfield that was between the Fairfield Public Library and my apartment. Getting into a line of two or three ahead of me, as I turned to look around to pass the time, I was somewhat unnerved to find that Peter had silently pulled up close to me, close enough to touch me. It wasn't his sudden, unexpected appearance that unnerved me, nor anything about his manner. When I had seen him earlier at the Fairfield Public Library, there had been nothing about his manner that was hostile or menacing as with the usual FBI targeting incidents. It was Peter's size along with his closeness that unnerved me. Peter was a larger man, wide across the chest, big shoulders. He seemed to loom over me. Had I not turned around, but taken only one step back, I would have bumped into him. He was that close.

Here too I had nothing I wanted to talk about with Peter. I turned away from him, and did not turn toward him again. I could see as I moved ahead in the line and turned sideways to place my grocers on the belt to move them to the cashier, Peter was no longer in the line. Yet, there was more encounter: As I was leaving the grocery stores, as automatic doors opened into a small lobby-like area between the large area of the store and outside, there was Peter again, standing facing me. Once more, I did not engage with him, and continued on my way out.

I saw Peter alive two, maybe three more times. As I was returning to my apartment after errands and library stops, I would see him walking vigorously along residential streets in my Black Rock neighborhood. He died in a vehicle accident between his CR-V and a Chrysler van on News Years Day 2020. The driver of the van told police he had "self-medicated" on drugs. Peter died in St. Vincent's Medical Center a couple of days later. The van driver was charged with manslaughter, and in 2022 was sentenced to 15 years in prison. There were aspects of the deadly incident raising suspicions in me that Peter, like Susan, was another victim of FBI psychopathology and malevolence. Among these was that I had been in touch with Peter two or three times in the December 2019 weeks before the end-of-year holidays to see about making an appointment with him after the holidays. Before contacting Peter at this time, I did online research to see if he was still in the area and working as a lawyer.

Once again, however, as in contacting Peter after the August and September 2015 incidents at the Pequot Library, I never heard from him. I'm sure, however, that with the FBI's constant monitoring of my phone calls and computer activity, it knew that I had been trying to reach him. At this time, December 2019, I was wanting to get in touch with Peter to see if he would be interested in representing me in prosecution of me for trespass at the Pequot Library. In June 2019, after witnessing lawsuits against Pequot Library, staff members, and Susan Ei replaced by Paul Zalon as estate executor after her death terminated after corruption by lawyers and judges and machinations among defendants, I had gone to Pequot Library knowing I would be arrested. I saw this as the best way to expose the crime and corruption that I had experienced and which had spread throughout the library and beyond. The case was so transparently weak that I thought Peter might be interested in representing me as defense lawyer getting the case quickly dismissed with following malicious prosecution civil litigation against the Pequot Library and certain employees. As it happened, with myself continuing to represent myself self-represented as it is called in Connecticut when a party in a legal case represents himself instead of having a lawyer, the trespass case was dismissed in May 2022 by the prosecutor and the judge at a hearing as a trial was imminent.

My suspicions over the death of Susan Ei led me to go to the town clerk's office of Fairfield to get a copy of her death certificate. Mainly, I was curious about the cause of death. But the death certificate was of interest to me as well because it was required if my lawsuit against her was to continue by substituting Susan Ei's husband Paul Zalon as defendant and administrator of her estate, a legal process involving the Fairfield probate court.

I had never seen, much less reviewed a death certificate before. I knew of course the basic information such as name and date of death would be in it. I didn't really know if cause of death would be cited in a publicly available death certificate such as the one I got a copy of at the town of Fairfield clerk's office in the town hall group of buildings. For all I knew this might be found only in hospital or family records which were private.

In an overview of the death certificate to take in its organization and some of the headings of its many boxes for information to be filled in by hand, I saw that the certificate began with Susan Ei's name, birth date, etc. and ended with the name of the doctor who confirmed the death just above the bottom line where a "registrar" filled in the date the certificate was received — April 3, 2017 — and wrote his signature.

Then scrutinizing the certificate to see what it might offer to have some understanding of the circumstances of Susan Ei's death, I found her date of birth, age when she died (64), and the names of her parents and her husband. I saw that she died at Norwalk Hospital at 2:25AM on March 31, 2017, the date given in the "suggestion of death" legal notice. I was startled, and grew even more suspicious about the cause of Susan Ei's death when I saw that she was cremated at a Bridgeport crematory on April 4, 2017. This was the date the "suggestion of death" notice had been filed by Susan Ei's lawyer in my lawsuit. Susan Ei had been dead and cremated before I got word of this.

In the "suggestion of death"notice, Susan Ei's lawyer states, "[D]efendant, Susan Ei, passed away of March 31, 2017. Counsel for the undersigned [Susan Ei, defendant] has filed this notice simultaneous to learning of Mrs. Ei's death." (The name was wrong. She was not Mrs. Ei, but Mrs. Zalon if she were going to use "Mrs."; though she went nearly always by her maiden name.) I wasn't the only one who got delayed notice on Susan Ei's death. Her lawyer was not informed of her death until four or five days later. March 31 was a Friday, April 4, the following Tuesday. The intervening weekend could account for the delay, though empty boxes in the death certificate raise questions about her death which in turn raise questions if the time and date of her death are accurate.

Box 38 of the death certificate is titled "Date pronounced dead", with "3/31/17" filled in; box 39, "time pronounced", with "2:25 am" filled in. Next along the same line is "38. Pronouncer's name and degree or title (print)". Box 38 is blank. Box "39. Pronouncer's signature" has a horizontal slash mark in it going across the tail, or descender, of the letter "g" of the name of the funeral director receiving Susan Ei's body for cremation in the box above, #34. The last box on the line is "40. Date signed", blank too.

The following boxes in the line below numbered 41, 42, 43 are for whether a medical examiner was contacted, whether an autopsy was performed, and whether the "autopsy findings were available to complete the cause of death" respectively. Small boxes for "no" in the first two are checked, with the last box, 43, left blank.

The "Cause of death" section, #44, has four lines, a through d, with a note "add additional lines if necessary." Susan Ei's death certificate gives the "IMMEDIATE CAUSE (final disease or condition resulting in death)" as "(a) hypoxic respiratory failure," noting with this in the column headed "approximate interval onset to death," "days," i. e., she developed this condition within days before dying. Underneath "IMMEDIATE CAUSE," is instructions, "Sequentially list conditions, if any, leading to the cause listed on line (a); Enter the UNDERLYING CAUSE (disease or injury that initiated the events resulting in death) LAST." On line (b) is, "severe pulmonary hypertension," with "weeks" in the column for "approximate interval onset to death." On line (c) is, "metastatic breast cancer, advanced," with "months" given in the column for "approximate interval onset to death."

Susan Ei's death certificate gives the "IMMEDIATE CAUSE (final disease or condition resulting in death)" as " (a) hypoxic respiratory failure," noting with this in the column headed "approximate interval onset to death," "days," i. e., she developed this condition with days before dying. Underneath "IMMEDIATE CAUSE," is instructions, "Sequentially list conditions, if any, leading to the cause listed on line (a); Enter the UNDERLYING CAUSE (disease or injury that initiated the events resulting in death) LAST." On line (b) is, "severe pulmonary hypertension," with "weeks" in the column for "approximate interval onset to death." On line (c) is, "metastatic breast cancer, advanced," with "months" given in the column for "approximate interval onset to death."

My medical knowledge as a doctor has is limited. Nonetheless, putting together different, but plainly interrelated facts as filled in by the doctor making out Susan Ei's death certificate and called for in the certificate as applicable, Susan Ei's death certificate indicates extreme, life-threatening, sudden physical conditions beginning at the time of my filing of the amended complaint on March 16, 2017, detailing her activities targeting me. March 16 to March 31, the date of death, is two weeks — corresponding to the "weeks" entered by the doctor in the "approximate interval onset to death" for "severe pulmonary hypertension."

I know Susan Ei could not have been ill with severe pulmonary hypertension serious enough to be hospitalized for this more than two weeks and probably less than this because I saw her stopped at a stop sign on Pequot Avenue in Southport center as I was stopped at a stop sign facing her after a regular stop at the Southport post office in days after I had filed the amended complaint on March 16, 2017. Susan Ei was driving her distinctive dark olive-green Honda SUV (larger than my Honda CR-V). No one else was in the car, and I saw her distinctly though I didn't stare. I don't know if she saw me. I presumed she was on her way to work since she was headed in the direction of the Pequot Library. If my presumption is correct, and she was going to work, this is further evidence that Susan Ei developed severe pulmonary hypertension serious enough to be hospitalized suddenly. I won't follow this line of inquiry further; but of note is the following from a website with information on severe pulmonary hypertension: "The survival of patients with pulmonary hypertension used to be around three to five years...." Yet according to her death certificate, Susan Ei had this condition for only "weeks." Of note as well, from another website, "Pulmonary hypertension is a type of high blood pressure."

Susan Ei's "hypoxic respiratory failure" afflicting her for only "days" can be examined with similar reasoning. "Respiratory" entails the lungs and relates to breathing. The immediate cause of Susan Ei's death was catastrophic failure of her respiratory system.

Susan Ei's death certificate indicates she was overcome suddenly with serious, life-threatening conditions affecting her lungs and respiratory system. The "underlying cause of death" is given as "metastatic breast cancer, advanced." The entry "months" for "approximate interval onset to death" is somewhat anomalous considering that "metastatic breast cancer, advanced" would take some time to develop to that point; and even if diagnosed months before Susan Ei's death at the end of March 2017 would be unlikely to be regarded as an underlying cause of death within the few months time. The following are a few pieces of information found online about metastatic breast cancer, advanced breast cancer spreading from the breast to other parts of the body: (i) The five-year survival rate for stage 4 breast cancer is 22 percent; median survival is three years; (ii) The median life expectancy for stage 4 mesothelioma is about 12 months; (iii) The American Cancer Society (ACS) states that the five-year survival rate after diagnosis for people with stage 4 breast cancer is 22 percent. Susan Ei's survival with metastatic breast cancer fell well short of the median.

Presumably Susan Ei did have breast cancer, though given the FBI's demonstrable witness intimidation included perjured statements no doubt coerced by such intimidation, and overt and implicit threats to numerous individuals besides me, this cannot be taken as certain. But putting this aside, and presuming Susan Ei did have breast cancer, it is highly unlikely it contributed to her death on March 31, 2017; which death was untimely and unexpected. I won't go into all of the online investigation I went into on the medical conditions, their causes, and their effects when seeing them listed in Susan Ei's death certificate. However, something turned up in a Google search regarding a connection between breast cancer and pulmonary hypertension goes further in raising questions about matters behind Susan Ei's death than ones already raised by my review of her death certificate. This online information I found is, "Can breast cancer cause pulmonary hypertension? Pulmonary tumor thrombotic microangiopathy (PTTM) is a rare, cancer-related, pulmonary complication that causes hypoxia, pulmonary hypertension, and heart failure. It rarely occurs in patients with metastatic or recurrent breast cancer." (National Library of Medicine National center of Biotechnology Information, from article published online, July 17, 2017)

The suddenness of Susan Ei's being overtaken and consequently shortly thereafter killed by the medical conditions listed as causes of death in her death certificate suggests a drug overdose or perhaps some condition resulting from extreme stress or perhaps a condition exacerbated by extreme stress so as to cause death. On their face, the causes of death in Susan Ei's death certificate do not explain her death, her untimely, sudden, and unexpected death. Her rapid cremation following her death preventing an autopsy or other type of investigation into the cause of her death such as a toxicology test strongly suggests someone has something to hide about the death of Susan Ei on March 31, 2017. Someone has a lot to hide.

12. Bribery, Advent of Stalking

This chapter on how bribery primes and perpetuates the FBI's targeting operations is chronologically out of order. The organization of the narrative is generally chronological as preferable to follow the development, interweavings, branchings, and headings of the various FBI activities as they enveloped various individuals and organizations. After a while in experiencing the facets and dimensions of the targeting and in conceiving this book in preparation for writing, I was able to piece together a multitude of incidents, individuals, intentions, and effects that happened over years. However, obviously with the FBI's subterfuge and covert activities, I was not able to perceive what was going on in every case or phase and all that was occurring as it was occurring. While I was able to and it was critical to me to recognize and be aware of FBI deceits, threats, and stratagems as I faced these day to day to avoid entrapment scenarios, not thoughtlessly say something that could be twisted to seem incriminating, be injured by a careless movement, or instinctively respond angrily or protectively so as to prompt an onslaught against me by someone or a group of individuals encircling me claiming self-defense on their part, I could not take in every detail of evert situation nor discern the pattern behind every incident.

Thus it was that I learned about the FBI bribery at the Pequot Library only some time after Susan Ei was dead. I do not remember when or how I saw the newsletter Pequot Library News 2016 with an article on renovation of the children's department headlined "Brown Bear, Brown Bear, What Do You See?" followed by the tag line "I see new carpeting! I see new sofas! I see children looking at me!" It may have been posted somewhere at the Library website; though I do not find newsletters posted there in my reviews of the site for this book. I my have seen it at the Library page on Facebook. I may have been sent an email copy. There is a place "Sign up for our eNewsletter" on the site now. If I've ever received eNewsletters, I don't remember. It's likely that my email was removed as a subscriber if I did subscribe.

However I came across the Pequot Library News 2016 newsletter, the article caught my attention as it the date of the "new carpeting," etc., 2016, was associated with the date Susan Ei's stalking of me began.

With the bad publicity Pequot Library and certain employees were getting from my social media postings, contact with politicians and journalists, and other activities as an investigative writer as I sometimes called myself, intimidation and coercion of Susan Ei alone would not do. (I say "investigative writer" rather than "investigative journalist" because I am not a professional journalist, and I am attached to no publication. I regard "investigative writer" as a type of citizen journalist.) Along with enlistment of Susan Ei and continuing intimidation and coercion of the Pequot Library employees I was identifying as having participated in the targeting incident so none would expose that it originated with the FBI, something more was now needed. The FBI would have to demonstrate that it was not completely indifferent to the library now being seen in a bad light from my social media postings and emails and it was not as feckless, reckless, and oafish as it was being shown to be. The FBI had a remedy for the damage it had brought to the Pequot Library. This remedy was bribery.

This bribery, not coincidentally, was mainly sprucing up the children's area of the Pequot Library. This bribery, not coincidentally, happened about the time Susan Ei began stalking me in the spring 2016 about the time I began my civil case against the Pequot Library and some of its staff in March.

The "Pequot Library News 2016," an issue of the library newsletter, has an article on the bribery. The headline of the article is, "Brown Bear, Brown Bear, What Do You See?", with the tag line "I see new carpeting! I see new sofas! I see children looking at me!" The complete text of the article on the upper half of one of the pages is, "After decades of active use, we are excited to see our Children's Department transform thanks to an anonymous donor, whose generosity helped launch a renovation. The donation has allowed us to purchase and install new carpeting, paint the walls and ceiling, apply wallpaper, and add three new, comfy blue couches. Through the creative talent of interior designer, Parker Rogers, owner of Parker & Co., and the Children's Renovation Committee, these organizations have transformed the space into an open, sun-filled area for relaxation, play, and learning.

"Unlike a municipal library which receives 100% of funding from the town, Pequot Library is a public association library, and relies on friends like Parker and you to help us provide our community with all the free and exciting services and programs we host each year.

"The Children's Department still needs new shelving, upgraded lighting, and more furniture before it it complete, all of which will cost over $75.000. Thank you for your continued gifts and for considering being a part of this new improved space, where children can grow, learn, and explore! Please contact Susan Ei, Children's Librarian at (203- 259-0346 ext. 16 or childrens[at]pequotlibrary.org to find out how you can help."

Parker & Co., owned by Parker Rogers, is a high-end interior design firm. Its office is at 411 Pequot Avenue, Southport, Connecticut — across from the Southport Post Office and about a quarter mile east of the Pequot Library. There is no evidence Parker Rogers or his company knew it was being involved in the FBI bribery at the Pequot Library. The case for FBI bribery is based on the circumstantial evidence of the timing of the renovation of the children's department of the Pequot Library with the start of Susan Ei's stalking of me, and the filing of my civil complaint against the Library and some staff. The circumstantial evidence of the connection between Susan Ei's absence as a defendant in my civil case indicating as far as I was able to see and to assume, she had not participated in the August 2015 targeting incident; her position as children's librarian; her stalking of me starting in April 2016; and the FBI's aim of control over Pequot Library employees to assure that none would expose the FBI criminality at the Library, points to FBI bribery. Sometimes intimidation, however heavy-handed and alarming, is not enough. Besides, as a ploy at times, the FBI tries to demonstrate to its stooges and dupes that it is not essentially nihilistic and depends on intimidation, coercion, and crime for its survival.

Whether or not the FBI believed it had in fact gotten to Susan Ei with defamatory lies about me and agreement to allow for or take part in a targeting incident of me or whether or not Susan Ei to some degree acceded to the FBI formation of a group of employees to take part in the targeting incident or rejected this utterly is not essential to the enlisting of Susan Ei to stalk me or the bribery of her, along with others at the Library, by the renovation of the children's department. For the FBI wanting determinative and assuring control of the situation and employees at the Pequot Library, the essential concern was that I witness and thus understand that the FBI had such control.

There is more evidence beyond this circumstantial evidence tied in with the Pequot Library. Since I had been barred from the library under threat of arrest for trespass, I would not know about the renovation. However, the Susan Ei stalking was not the only sign that the FBI was expanding its targeting of me by adding new facets.

In the few months after I filed my civil case in March 2016, there were several incidents at different locations impressing on me, as intended, that the FBI was bribing individuals at these locations, and by extension in some cases, bribing an organization by providing services and gifts.

The first place where I was made aware that something was going on the FBI wanted me to be aware of was the Fairfield Public Library. About the time of the renovation of the Pequot Library children's department funded by an anonymous donor — which renovation I did know about at the time — there were parts of the Fairfield Public Library being painted as I saw in stops there at this time. These were sections of walls, mostly along the long, sloping walkway between the magazine room on the upper level and the main level with the copying machine, desks where patrons can work, reference desk, and other services and facilities and also the walls surrounding the copying machine, setting it off from the large open space with the work desks and the reference desk.

I not only saw that painting was going on with younger men painting the walls, but I was intentionally made aware that the painting was going on by being inconvenienced by it two times at different spots. As the FBI knew from its surveillance for tailoring its harassment and menacing of me, after pulling out the section of the daily New York Times with the crossword puzzle in the magazine room, I would carry it to the copying machine on the lower level down the sloping ramp. Before going to the copying machine, I would stop at a spot along the ramp to place the section on the wide panel at the top of the sloping wall to open it and fold it so the crossword could be copied at the copying machine. One day when the painting was going on, as I was at the wall opening and folding the paper, suddenly a man with a paint roller came down the slope moving toward me. A couple of feet to my left, he started painting the wall with the roller, and moving toward me. All of a sudden, he had decided to paint the section of the wall where I was standing. He moved toward me somewhat aggressively, with no indication that he was going to pause so I could finish folding the newspaper section. I moved away from where I was, and finished folding the section by the copy machine.

Another day, after I had finished folding the section with the crossword puzzle and was at the copying machine ready to copy the puzzle, all of a sudden a man with a paint roller came around the wall enclosing the copying machine and started to paint the section of the wall right beside me. The space between the left side of the copying machine and the part of the wall he wanted to paint was only about a foot and a half. The man had to reach into this space too narrow to stand in. He reached at my left, partly behind me, seeming to strain to reach the part of the wall he wanted to paint and annoyed that I was not allowing him to get closer to this part so he would reach it easier. I immediately moved out of the way, before I had copied the crossword puzzle. I waited until the man finished his charade of painting the section of the wall I happened to have been interfering with. A moment after interrupting me, the man stopped the painting, and moved away. As with the earlier interruption of me along the sloping walkway, this interruption related to painting. Neither instance however was related to any work of painting anything more than a small section of wall I happened to be standing at one two different days when at the Fairfield Public Library.

I never saw any painting project being done at the Fairfield Public Library about the time the renovation unbeknownst to me at the time was going on at the Pequot Library children's department and Susan Ei began stalking me. At the time, to me, the two contrived incidents involving painting sections of walls at the Fairfield Public Library with the somewhat aggressive movements of the men with paint rollers was seen as more FBI harassment and menacing. After Pequot Library custodian Robert Repko's attention-getting appearance at the Fairfield Public Library and Susan Ei's stalking of me, I saw the contrived painting incidents as latest incidents in the FBI's semiotics of terrorism. After my having filed my case against Pequot Library and certain employees, the FBI was intensifying its harassment and menacing activities against me.

There was a third incident involving painting. This one happened at my second-floor apartment in the Black Rock area of Bridgeport. As I came home one afternoon, as I was nearing the top of the stairs to the landing outside my door, I saw painting supplies at the right side of the top step and the adjacent area of the landing, at the end of the railing across part of the landing. There was a tray dotted with dried paint, a small paint can, and some rags. As I got to the landing avoiding the painting materials, across the six-foot-wide landing was a man sitting on a tarp painting the lower part of a two-tone painted wall of the landing. The lower part was a dark green, the upper part, light green, a pattern going through the walls of the landings and stairways of the apartments in this area of the building.

The man turned his upper body toward me and looked at me as I got fully on to the landing and was making the few steps to my front door. I had seen him two or three times over the past week or so on the grounds of the group of four apartment buildings in the complex. He hadn't been doing any work, and he wasn't dressed as a workman. He had crossed my pathway, not close, but close enough so that I would recognize him. It was the same man I saw outside the two or three times, and now saw right outside the door to my apartment, painting.

Thus when perusing the Pequot Library website one day as I occasionally did to see what was going on there lately since I had been barred from the scene of the crime, looking through the "Pequot Library News 2016," newsletter, coming to the short "Brown Bear, Brown Bear, What Do You See?" article and reading through it, the passage "The donation has allowed us to purchase and install new carpeting, paint the walls and ceiling, apply wallpaper...." "Paint the walls"?! My eyes grew large, my head jerked. "Paint the walls"?! I read the phrase over and over. "Paint the walls." I then saw that the scenarios I had encountered at the Fairfield Public Library and at the door of my apartment were not scenarios involving painting as a pretext for coming near to me and interacting with me to harass me and add to my sense of alarm in being viciously and continuously targeted, but that the painting element of the scenarios was key to grasping what the FBI was meaning to convey to me they were effecting at the Pequot Library at the time.

Since I was prohibited from going to the Pequot Library under threat of trespass and thus would not see the renovations of the children's department going on in the spring 2016 and deduce that the renovation was FBI bribery from the timing of the renovation and the connection between the children's department where it was being done and children's librarian Susan Ei who during this time began stalking me, the FBI had to devise scenarios that were not just menacing reminders that I was being targeted, but which were symbolic in a way that the repeated, familiar scenarios were not. The connection between the paint rollers and other painting paraphernalia that was pushed into my notice at the Fairfield Public Library and at my apartment and the report of painting as part of the Pequot Library children's department renovation in spring 2016 would be too apparent to deny.

The Pequot Library renovation was not the only bribery the FBI was involved in. At different times, FBI agents proudly and ostentatiously purchased large quantities of wine at the Fairfield wine shop where Susan Ei had stalked me in one incident; in one such incident, a woman agent announcing to one of the owners who was at the cash register, "We'll be back for more." This incident was accompanied by one of the two young male agents who were with her closing in on me suddenly and somewhat aggressively so I would move aside as he made believe he was wanting to look at something on the counter. Another time, at a copy shop near the Fairfield Public Library which I was using at the time to run off legal papers, as the FBI knew from surveillance, as I was standing at the counter waiting for the young woman clerk to finish a copying job for me, a younger man walked in carrying a large bouquet of flowers in a basket. He left them on the counter and nodded his head toward the woman clerk to let he know the bouquet was for her, from the FBI. I presume the bribery in this case of the copy shop was so the woman clerk would let the FBI know what I was running off.

The FBI continued its bribery beyond the death of Susan Ei in March 2017. As I saw in my occasional perusals of the Pequot Library website in later years, there was a revision of the website thanks to an "anonymous donor" among others. All the categories for donations at different financial levels for the new roof put on the Library in 2021 found in this year's newsletter list an "anonymous" donor. In witnessing the length of time certain individuals and certain organizations continue to participate in the targeting, I see that these must be objects of the FBI's bribery too. Being involved in the targeting program for so long and acting in such unnatural ways when they see I am seeing them in grocery stores, along a sidewalk, and elsewhere over such a period of time must require inducement beyond simply request by the FBI. As the FBI works to harmfully target those it regards as unworthy according to whatever bizarre criteria it uses for this, so does the FBI reward and favor those it regards as worthy in its social engineering.

13. Slipping Away

The individual who knows the most about Susan's last days and the causes of her death is her husband Paul Zalon.

Paul Zalon is a successful entrepreneurial businessperson in Fairfield, Connecticut. He is the owner of Spark Studios. Sparks Studios designs and markets what might be described as inspired gadgets, i. e., mostly useless gadgets which are nonetheless desirable for their inventiveness and visual appeal which can enhance the atmosphere of an occasion, make it memorable, and be a memento. The Studios makes "custom promotional items" for leading theme parks such as Disneyland, cruise lines, museums, and specialty chains on order from them for special occasions, seasonal sales, and branding campaigns. Small toys, stationary items such as pens, coffee mugs, and frames for photos are among the types of items Sparks Studios designs for clients, which are mostly upscale institutions or major popular culture companies. Although the items such as coffee mugs or pens are common, Sparks Studios makes each unique for its purpose for a client by incorporating into such common items some form of electronics making the item especially flashy and animated.

Paul Zalon has a MFA from Yale in stage design/architecture, and before that earned a B.A. in biology and theater design at New York University. The combination of biology and theater design in his NYU undergraduate degree is unusual. But the symbiosis of these subjects is reflected in the Sparks Studio's creations which combine design with animated effects created by their electronics, lighting, sounds, or movement. That many of Sparks Studios creations are patented testifies to the uniqueness as products and use of electronics and other factors in the designs. From 1976 to 1978 Paul Zalon was an adjunct professor of theater design at Princeton. Sparks Studios was founded in 2009, and today has offices in China presumably to see to production of its creations and shipment of them to clients.

I didn't know Paul Zalon. I didn't know Susan Ei was married to him. I learned Susan had at least one daughter at one of Pequot Library's annual summer book sales. At the end of this particular year's sale was a book auction. Book-sale volunteers were helping interested buyers by bringing books going to be auctioned to tables which were set up for the buyers to look them over. As I

learned by seeing Susan speak to her, one of the volunteers was a daughter of
hers. It was years later when I learned that Susan and Paul Zalon had two
daughters upon reading obituaries for Susan. It as in the obituaries too that I
learned that Susan and Paul Zalon were married.

Although I didn't know Paul Zalon and Susan Ei were married, I had seen him
three times at Pequot Library without knowing his name. He had been there to
see Susan. Each time, he had seen me. In one instance, as Susan was standing at
the back door of the library looking out at the man I have since learned was Paul
Zalon standing at the open door of his BMW apparently after having spoken with
Susan in the library, I walked up the ramp to the door and passed closely by
Susan, so that for a moment, Susan and I were together in Paul Zalon's line of
sight.

The two other times Paul Zalon saw me I was in the same vicinity of the library as
Susan. I was sitting at a computer in the children's section which I often did
because I could sit down instead of stand at one of the other library computers for
patrons in the hallway, and often the hallway computers were in use. At the times
I used the computers in the children's section, it was quiet and empty except for
Susan and me. When the children's section was quiet and empty of any children
was an ideal time for Paul Zalon to come to see Susan. Each of the two times Paul
Zalon was at the library to see Susan, he walked past me sitting only about five
feet away to his right —and he looked at me. I suppose his unusual measure of
coming to the Library was to see Susan because of some trouble in their
relationship. Spouses or any relatives of staff rarely came to the library, where
staff would be working and the appearance of spouse or other relative would
inevitably raise questions. Since the children's section was away from the main
part of the library where staff would be at the circulation desk or moving about in
their work tasks and could be entered by the back door, Paul Zalon using this
door came and went in his stops to see Susan unseen by staff, and probably
unseen except by Susan and me in the two times I saw him inside the library to
see Susan.

I assume that since I had seen Paul Zalon two times inside the library and the
once outside the library next to his BMW presumably leaving after having seen
Susan inside, he had been to the library at least with Susan's tacit approval. Who
knows how many other times he may have been there to see Susan? It was none
of my business. I may have become some part of Paul Zalon's business however
since I assume he had come to the library to see Susan because of some trouble
that had arisen in their relationship. Since Paul Zalon saw me three times in

proximity to Susan, he may have suspected there was something between us. There wasn't. We knew each other — which was little more than recognizing each other — because we would see each other all the time when we were both at the library at the same time. Even if Susan were in the children's section doing something when I was at the library, she would see me when I was at the copy machine running of the day's N. Y. Times crossword puzzle or some business papers. Apart from this, Susan and I would often see each other when she was out to the circulation desk in the main part of the library to see a staff member there about something or taking a break from what she was doing in the children's section. I never had a conversation with Susan, and as I say didn't know much about her beyond that she was a fixture at the library for a long time and had been appointed children's librarian at some point. Susan always had a coolness toward me, kept a distance, whereas I had friendly and in some cases cordial relationships with some staff, knowing about their husbands and their children. I now think Susan kept a distance because we saw each other so frequently and she was married.

The husband Paul Zalon knows more about details of Susan Ei's final days. He knows more about her emotional states, developing medical problems leading to admissions at Norwalk Hospital, any psychiatric problems cropping up, medications available to her, relations with her daughters, relatives, friends, and Pequot Library staff — and relations with her FBI handlers. It is inconceivable that Susan would not have told him something about her involvement with the FBI after my filing of my amended complaint going into details of the series of stalking incidents. Undoubtedly Paul Zalon would have read the amended complaint. Inquiring of Susan what was going on after having done so — assuming he didn't already know about Susan's involvement with the FBI — there would have been no other explanation for Susan's stalking actions. She was not one to all of a sudden, even considering the August 2015 gang-stalking/social cleansing targeting incident of me at the Pequot Library, to begin stalking me, knowing just where I was and leaving wherever she was to come to stand plainly noticeably close to me gazing in my direction.

Loyalty to Pequot Library fellow and sisters employees whose treacherous actions against me in concert with FBI agents alone did not account for an escalating series of stalking incidents at two different locations intended to and designed to unnerve me and impress upon me I was in dire circumstances. The Pequot Library employees' duplicity had already been exposed. Any actions by Susan at this point would have been not to prevent the exposure, but to intimidate me not to pursue my lawsuit with the possibility of discovering and exposing additional, graver treacheries and conclusively on the bases of documents and testimony proving that the FBI was the source of what had transpired. Susan's stalking was in the vein of the court papers with the red blotches looking like blood sent to me in conjunction with my filing the case against the library and certain employees and the military-style baseball cap with the death's head on it placed outside the door of my apartment, unarguably another death threat. Susan's stalking actions followed by allowing the use of her car to be parked near my apartment where I could not miss seeing it were qualitatively different from the lies Pequot Library employees resorted to to hope to disguise their involvement in the library targeting incident. With the stalking, Susan had become physically and for a longer period of time and at locations a distance from the library involved in the FBI malevolence and treachery, and so had become an FBI accomplice in such a way that her actions were differentiated from those of the others whose duplicities and roles were confined to the library. Susan had engaged in actions that were totally out of character for her. The FBI was the only explanation.

That the FBI had rendered Susan an accomplice who was not embedded in the interlacing of lies and conspiratorial network at the library left Susan abandoned, exposed in a way the others were not when the Federal judge ruled that my civil case started in Connecticut state court would not be consolidated with the case against the library and some employees that had been removed to Federal court, but was remanded back to state court. None of the Pequot Library employees' lies and distortions would offer cover for Susan. Nor was Susan enclosed by, and thus somewhat covered by the mesh of mutually reinforcing lies of the other Pequot Library employees who had been a part of the FBI scheme. Although I and the employees knew that the lies and the conspiracy could be exposed in a public forum such as a trial, such a forum could not be reached without somewhat complex, protracted procedure. And the FBI by intimidation of judges, witness tampering, subornation of perjury, and other corruption and criminal activity was subverting this procedure.

The FBI subverted procedure in my case against Susan Ei too. But this did not offer Susan the feeling of being protected by the FBI the other employees had in believing the FBI was all powerful. Nor did the FBI's subversion create for the time a gulf between my allegations and proof of them in Susan's cases as this did in the Pequot Library case. The insult to Susan was that her actions had been described and so exposed in my amended complaint. And these were far beyond and different from the actions of Adair Heitmann and Denise Martin at the Pequot Library in the August 2015 targeting incident which though unseemly and opening them to liability, occurred at their workplace, were relatively brief, and did not require much outside of their normal work activity. By contrast, in going far outside of her workplace, engaging in a series of stalking incidents at different places over a few months, and then loaning her car to the FBI to extend the range and manner of menacing me, Susan demonstrated a commitment to the FBI's maliciousness much beyond that demonstrated by anyone else at the Pequot Library, and so appeared to demonstrate a hostility toward me and wish to unnerve and menace me she shared with the FBI. This was what seemed plain; and while there was much more to what transpired with Susan in the hands of the FBI, this was murky, ambiguous, puzzling.

Paul Zalon could offer little consolation to Susan under the circumstances. The FBI had failed in buffering her from my descriptions of her actions as recounted in my amended complaint. The FBI had failed in affording her the feeling of security afforded by belonging to a group, in this case the group of Pequot Library employees who were defendants in my case against them and the library. Knowing that by her stalking she had done something that was inexplicable and inexcusable, Susan could find no succor in her daughters. Susan telling herself she had been a good mother who had raised daughters to be proud of was no solace to her when she knew she had engaged in actions and been involved in destructive relationships she had raised them to be smart enough and humane enough to avoid. Susan had created vulnerabilities for herself which could not be salved, and she had caused injuries to her relationships and to her career, and to her self-regard and image of herself too, which she knew could not be remedied. She was on her own

Although there was nothing meaningful Paul Zalon could do to shore up Susan's collapsed self-regard, her multifarious acute pains, he did take one action which he hoped might bring some alleviation for Susan's painful situation. At one time between when my amended complaint appeared on the Bridgeport Superior Court case docket following the remand by the Federal Court and when Susan and I had the brief encounter in Southport center at the stop signs as we were driving in different directions, when I was in the Southport post office at the table in the foyer riffling through my mail, Paul Zalon came in. By now I knew he had some relationship with Susan having seen him with her at the Pequot Library; although I did not yet know he was her husband. He took the couple of steps from doorway to where I was standing, positioning himself about a foot from me to my right. I glanced partly sideways mainly to acknowledge his presence and my awareness of the situation. I had recognized who he was in glancing toward the doorway when I heard it open. He stood motionless and silent for about twenty-five seconds. It may have been somewhat longer. He stood by me looking at me. I glanced toward him again, seeing his face. I wanted to get a look at his eyes. His eyes registered nothing that I could make out, only that he was looking at me. He looked steadily at me the whole time, but I wouldn't say this was intently.

Paul Zalon's appearance at the Southport post office and his standing next to me for the part of a minute was undoubtedly to let me know he was informed about my lawsuit against his wife. But I had presumed this, and I see no reason why he would not have presumed that I had. So I expect his aim in seeking me out upon being told no doubt by someone with the FBI I was at the post office and coming in and standing beside me for a stretch of a number of seconds was to convey to me that there was more that I would or should want to know other than the status and stage of my lawsuit. This would be, of course, that his wife was in some plight, entailing supposedly that their marital relationship was being disrupted and that Susan was distressed. These too I had presumed though, although I can suppose Paul Zalon, not knowing me at all, could have believed that I was not aware of the magnitude of disruption and distress.

I was, as I had all along, been aware of the volatile nature of the matters I was dealing with, with probable and in many respects predictable repercussions for different individuals, including myself. Considering the risks I was talking on and the threats, hostilities, and defamations I had met with and continued to meet with in pressing for my basic rights and in all areas of my life including business, I was only so sympathetic with the position, with the plight, of any individual who was a part of the threats, etc.; even Susan Ei who I recognized was one of the best and most admirable persons working at Pequot Library. For me, the situation broadly with all that it encompassed and implied and with respect to particulars for any individual of the many involved was not simply or basically that no one was showing me sympathy even though they all knew I was the aggrieved party who was being put at risk by a perverse, pathological FBI. I'm not one to seek nor to expect sympathy. Rather, I hope for reasonable understanding and fairness, though I was finding neither. All that I was finding in my efforts to publicize what was going on and secure my rights and receive relevant recompense was escalating and widening instances and networks of threats, hostilities, and defamations. Susan Ei's stalking was a prime example of this.

Paul Zalon is a somewhat burly man with somewhat tangled long hair and sproutings of a beard across his lower face. As he stood beside me as the seconds went by, the situation concomitantly seemed to develop a density and weight. I was not alarmed. I suppose he meant for me to say something, for us to have some sort of communication. I was not moved to say anything to him, and nothing came to mind. Anything I would say to him would be unpleasant for him. I would have no good news for Susan.

I waited, continuing to look through my mail, at the same time acknowledging not only his presence, but that I knew who he was. Since it was soon apparent that I had nothing to say, I thought he would say something. I did nothing to discourage this. I didn't move anywhere nor shrink from him. The twenty-five or so seconds went by without him saying a word to me either. Paul Zalon turned and left.

Paul Zalon and Susan Ei had been married for at least about twenty years. At the time the daughters were both about twenty years old, one a little younger, the other a little older. They had been married long enough that there would not have to have been much conversation between them for each to realize the gravity of Susan's plight. Susan was like a rock sinking into a horizonless sea, her sorrows drifting by her like flotsam. As keenly as she felt them, she could not relate to them, they were so strange. She never imagined she would have felt such sorrows in her life. They were not the customary sorrows she had often heard about and expected and at times experienced from her humanity — the death of loved ones, the mistakes of children, estrangement from husbands and close friends, tragedies. Her sorrows were alien, and as such were like chemicals dissolving her person. She could not relate to them; she could not recognize herself in them. There were no rituals or environment for soothing them, for bringing her back from her sinking, fragmentation, and deterioration.

Paul Zalon was witness to Susan's downward spiral. As there were no rituals or environment to offer her comfort and renewal, there were no words he could say to provide this, nor even provide hope of comfort or renewal. By agreeing to be a major player in the FBI's demented program of targeting me entailing harassment and menacing, Susan had cut herself off from her past life. In so doing, she had cut herself off from all relationships, public image, and self-conception she had established in her life, her former life, as these had been. Her relationship with Paul Zalon would never be the same. Despite his sincere efforts to support and console Susan, he would be an observer to what was going on with her in her last days.

Susan was not only disconsolate, she was unconsolable. Her standards were too high. She knew what these were despite her breach of them. She was too honest to accept pale rationalizations or contrived vacuous justifications. Even in her misery, she was too proud and self-respecting to plead for understanding or forgiveness. She was too independent to look to or expect anyone else to provide for her what she could not provide for herself. She had lived as Susan Ei, she would die as Susan Ei, the name on her birth certificate, the name on her death certificate.

Husband Paul Zalon was present to each of the levels of Susan Ei's descent into the dark depths of hopelessness — the first filing of my complaint with its sketchy references to the stalking and alarm and anxieties it caused in me as it was intended; the months of waiting for a ruling from Federal Court on whether my civil case against her would be consolidated with my Pequot Library case in Federal court; the shock of the Federal Court ruling that the case was remanded to state court; the concomitant filing of my amended complaint with its details of times, locations, and Susan's stationing of herself and her movements in the stalking instances and the account that her metallic green Honda SUV had been parked several times outside my Black Rock apartment to extend, escalate, and intensify the FBI's activities to harass, menace, and unsettle me; the agonizing ambiguities entailed in not knowing who knew what about her involvement with the FBI and stalking me as part of its targeting program from seeing my amended complaint at the state judicial website or talk among people who knew Susan making her daily activities and all her relationships uneasy by feeling tentative and false; the daughters' inevitable disappointments, questions, and puzzles about their mother; disruptions to the husband's and the daughters' relationships with others widening the range of injuries done like ripples in a pond, Susan's stalking actions the stone tossed into the previously placid surface; Susan's increasing sense of being caught in a maze of misplaced confidence in others, misreading of fundamentals of the situation — mainly that I was not going to be intimidated and threatened without defending myself and that the FBI is unscrupulous — and knowledge of her own mistakes and deluded decisions; Susan's life drifting away from her; the tugging at the bonds that had grown between husband and wife as Susan slipped deeper into the depths until the bonds broke. For Susan, death appeared like an answer, like a deliverance, when she got to the point, the stage of descent, where outside world seemed grotesquely distorted, too strange to navigate or even negotiate, inside world seemed swept away, vanished, irretrievable, taunting.

On April 4, 2017, less than 24 hours after Susan's body was released from Norwalk Hospital, she was cremated at a crematorium on South Pine Creek Road, Fairfield, Connecticut. By the time I learned about this in a court document filed by her defense attorney that I was notified about, there were only ashes.

14. Loose Ends

There is no doubt the FBI infiltrated the Pequot Library and coerced several staff
members to participate in targeting of me. There is no doubt Susan Ei stalked me
at the Southport post office and Harry's Wine and Liquor Market in Fairfield, and
no doubt that her distinctive metallic-green Honda Odyssey appeared three or
four times parked at the group of apartment buildings in the area of Bridgeport
known as Black Rock where I rent an apartment in a parking space where I could
not help but see it when I went to my Honda CR-V. There is no doubt I filed a
lawsuit against Susan Ei, and no doubt that at a particular juncture of this lawsuit
where Susan Ei was left feeling very vulnerable and probably to some degree
alarmed and frightened in that this lawsuit was separated from my lawsuit
against the Pequot Library as an institution and certain staff members, a woman
in her late 20s or early 30s stood at the counter of the clerk's office at the
Bridgeport Superior Court and said loudly with me standing about six feet away
that "this was getting really serious" at the very time my lawsuit against Susan Ei
had become separated from my other lawsuit.

There is no doubt Susan Ei died not long after I had heard that "this was getting
really serious." There is no doubt Susan Ei's husband Paul Zalon came to the
Southport post office to encounter me, and stand silently beside me with me
barely acknowledging him. I wasn't meaning to be rude or to be ignoring him. I
just didn't know what to say. For me, the circumstances and many legal, social,
and moral issues raised by the circumstances, which circumstances were created
by the FBI, were what were most relevant and significant, not Susan Ei, any of the
staff at the Pequot Library, nor even me. My actions and ends taking on risk by
me, and as I came to realize, more risk than I at first expected or imaged, were to
expose what I experienced and realized about law-enforcement, the legal system,
and government so that citizens could not only be forewarned about this and thus
able to protect themselves and others from such malevolence and perversity, but
also to do what they might be interested in doing to insure or better the state and
workings of decent, democratic society.

The number, ties, and focus of the events and particulars in the untimely death of
Susan Ei leave one in no position other than seeing that her death was not
natural, i. e., did not occur according to the natural unfolding of aspects of her
life, including her medical condition of breast cancer reported in some media

articles on her death, but which may have been put out as a part of the cover-up of events, individuals, facts, and curious timeline surrounding her death. In any event, if Susan did have breast cancer, this would have been aggravated by the pressures she was under from having consigned herself to be an FBI operative by stalking me. Such aggravation would have destabilized Susan physically, emotionally, and psychologically to a greater degree than breast cancer alone would have. As her death certification states, the breast cancer was advanced, and therefore not recent. Susan would have accommodated it in some way, even if not have become fully or considerably adjusted to it. She would not and could not have however expected or been in any position to accommodate the duplicities and betrayals of the FBI she came to realize as my lawsuit progressed. The FBI cannot disassociate itself from Susan's deteriorating condition and her untimely death — the FBI can only work to cover up its connection to Susan's death.

In trying to tie together the loose ends of my long and changing relationship with Susan Ei and present facts relating to her death that remained unknown, though not necessary in drawing a relevant, persuasive picture of the factors going in to her death, I at one time emailed her husband Paul Zalon at his email at the website of his business, and also emailed his daughters who at the time were living in the upper Midwest. I did not hear from any of them, as expected. As with so many others, the FBI would have "advised" them that it was not in their interest to be in touch with me; when what the FBI was actually getting at was that it was not in the FBI's interest for them to be in touch with me.

There is no doubt that Susan Ei's family members would have revealing and poignant things to say. Susan was gone so suddenly. It is not only the suddenness of the loss of her, but also the loss of her spirit, brightness, and commitment to the Pequot Library and Southport that are missed, and turn ones who knew her to fond and regretful recollections of her. She was gone too soon, and unnecessarily.

The family members could add some evidence to the circumstances of Susan's death, and probably, especially the husband, of the origin, nature, details, and timeline of Susan's course with the FBI and her eventual despair, despair so profound and tormenting death seemed like freedom.

The information the family members of the husband and the two daughters could undoubtedly provide is not essential to the case of the FBI's involvement in the death of Susan Ei making for the timeline and the series of incidents in this. The family members could in all probability provide information on changes in Susan's behavior and emotional state, and perhaps her relationship with her FBI handlers; but the facts are apparent, documented, and compelling on their own.

The facts as known make for probable cause. I've made the case as far as I can go with my limited resources, capacities as a private citizen and investigator, and participant as a witness. I have not however given up on my efforts to gather more evidence as I am able and to follow lines of possible additional developments and evidence collection which remain or come about as sparse as these may be, and becoming more and more sparse as time goes by.

In addition to the undeniable timeline and course of incidents leading to Susan's death on March 30, 2017, strongly suggesting FBI responsibility for her death, there are certain other documents which would shed more light on the final month, days, and hours of Susan's life. These are especially, as I see it, medical documents. For instance, documents pertaining to how Susan got to Norwalk Hospital would be relevant. Did she go there directly from her house on Pequot Avenue in Southport, or from somewhere else, such as an intermediate medical facility? Did her husband take her to Norwalk Hospital? If not, there would be ambulance or EMS, emergency vehicle records if this was how she got to the hospital. Was there a medical emergency? or was she just feeling out of sorts, perhaps seriously depressed, and her husband or some physician advised a hospital stay?

Any phone calls, especially a 911 call, made preceding the time when Susan went to Norwalk Hospital would be relevant as well. It goes without saying that hospital admission records would be informative, along with records of Susan's time in the hospital before her death in the early hours of March 31, 2017. The name of the individual who found Susan had died or reported her death curiously missing from her death certificate in the space for this is something that should be answered too. Medical records are notably difficult to obtain, even by lawyers and law-enforcement. There's nothing I can do on my own to examine these to get answers to fill in the blanks on matters regarding Susan's death.

Also of interest is medication that would have been available to Susan with respect to her breast cancer as recorded on her death certificate as an underlying or contributing cause of her death. I have encountered so many lies and deceits in the targeting of me and my related investigative efforts to delve into the operations of this and identify individuals and organizations responsible for it or participating in it as accomplices that there is little I take at face value with regard to Susan's death. Everything, including specifics of her death certificate, the reason she entered Norwalk Hospital, and why she was precipitously cremated has to be questioned.

Since I suspect that Susan committed suicide or perhaps died from an overdose of medication, or maybe even was poisoned when she was a patient at the hospital in a diabolical FBI scheme, with the hasty cremation being the strongest evidence for this, any medications available to Susan, prescribed to her, or administered at the hospital are of interest forensically.

There are loose ends in the case of the death of Susan Ei. But these loose ends do not make for the proverbial bucket of worms or tangled knot that is so confusing that it is virtually unsolvable. The loose ends in the case of Susan Ei's death are more like missing pieces of a puzzle. The picture is not complete. But there is no doubt there is a picture. The pieces of it put together to make as much of it as possible are evident. The subject of the picture is known.

Susan Ri's untimely, suspicious death followed by a hasty cremation and scattered evidence of a cover-up such as blanks in the death certificate is the subject of the puzzle. Missing pieces may be found over the passage of time as individuals knowing facts or circumstances about her death may come forward; individuals connected to Susan such as her FBI handlers bringing about her death or individuals, possibly Susan's husband, who know who the handlers were divulge what they know; employees and board members at the Pequot Library or friends of hers speak out; as improbable as this would be, Fairfield police begin investigating Susan's death as a crime; and identifiable individuals such as Susan's husband and likely others unknown at this time who undoubtedly know things about Susan's death and her physical and mental state in the couple of weeks and days preceding it decide to be open; and individuals in Southport, Fairfield, and surrounding communities where Susan had friends and engaged in activities loose their fear of FBI targeting and reprisals if they help to solve the crime.

If I knew what else I could do to move further along in solving the crime of Susan Ei's death, I would do it despite the risks in addition to ones I have faced already.

15. The House on the Hill

Susan lived in an older house at the top of a hill not far from the center of Southport, eastward toward Fairfield. There are steep concrete steps leading up to it from the road, to the porch running across the front of it. At the top of the hill slanting away from Pequot Avenue, Southport's main road which the house faced, and surrounded by trees and vegetation, its dimensions could not be taken fully in. To the right of the house facing it from Pequot Avenue was an open area of large cobblestones. This was the parking area, with steps leading from it up to the side door. Off from it farther into the property was a building which at one time may have been a garage and was since used as a shed. In front of it was a garden. Susan was an avid gardener.

The house was not impressive or imposing, with no attempts such as shiny new paint, jutting additions, or systematic landscaping to make it try to be. Rather it appeared comfortable and inviting, natural, like Susan. My thought on the house was that it was one of the older ones in Southport built like a country house at an early time when Southport was country.

I knew 122 Pequot Avenue was Susan's house because I had often seen her distinctive metallic-green Honda Odyssey parked in the cobblestone parking area at the side of the house when I drove past on my way from the Route 95 exit to the Southport post office to check mail, sometimes followed by a stop at the Pequot Library. I always liked having a look at the house when passing by because of my interest in local history.

One day in the spring of 2021, after I had disposed of my Honda CR-V for environmental and financial reasons and also to get into walking again as my favorite exercise, after having checked for mail at my post office box, I decided to walk to the Fairfield railroad station to catch a train back to Black Rock instead of my usual practice of going to the Southport station only about one hundred yards from the post office. In thinking about the route and the time it would take, I realized that I would pass by the house where Susan had lived.

For some reason, this struck me as a good idea although it wasn't the primary intent of my decision to walk to the Fairfield station about a mile east of Southport center. This was immediately followed by me wondering why the thought of walking by Susan's house to get a closer look hadn't come to me before. It wasn't that far from the Southport post office — less than half a mile, and I could have done this almost any day I had been to Southport even though I didn't do this so often as when I had had my SUV. I figured I was somewhat surprised that a walk by the house hadn't come to mind even though I regularly thought about her suspicious death and what might come up to move the situation forward to resolution was because while I hadn't given up hope, I wasn't optimistic.

My first walk by the house was uneventful. The husband's dark blue BMW was in the cobblestone area near the stairs up to the side door. With the house set on the hill back from the road and surrounded by trees and shrubbery, the scene was always quiet, pleasant, like looking at a field or patch of woods. Knowing that the daughters had moved to the upper Midwest to pursue careers as indicated by their LinkedIn profiles, I presumed that the husband was now the only occupant.

Enjoying my first walk to the Fairfield railroad station, I occasionally followed this up with other walks. With Susan's house right along the way, I always had a look. The husband's BMW was always parked in the cobblestone area in what looked to me to be the same spot, a few paces from the steps. I'm sure he went out once in a while, but not during the midday period when I was by about three times every two months during nice weather.

After my first two or three walks, things began to change with respect to the house. Nothing about the house itself changed — same appearance, husband's BMW parked at the side, same disheveled shrubbery. But there were noticeable changes in the street by the house, and on a few occasions activity on the property that no doubt related to my walks by the house.

It was evident my walks had attracted the notice of the FBI. I had long ago become familiar with the agency's signs that it had me under surveillance, which signs were meant also as witness intimidation of me. Cars parked on the road across from the house and sometimes on the same side of the road in front of the house next to Susan's going toward Southport center. There would be individuals sitting in these parked where there was no reason to be parked other than for the FBI to communicate to me that it was aware that I was walking by Susan's house and having a look at it when going by on my way to the Fairfield railroad station.

I can't imagine that the FBI thought I would gain any evidence simply by walking by. I supposed that the FBI was likely meaning to deter me from going on to the property and contacting Paul Zalon by knocking on the side door; which I never had any intention of doing. After having emailed Paul Zalon once or maybe two times, and having emailed the daughters using LinkedIn contact information, I gave up trying to get in touch with the surviving relatives. I didn't want to take the chance of arrest for harassment or some other crime the FBI would fabricate against me, as they with the cooperation of Pequot Library staff had fabricated the trespass complaint against me. I was also concerned that if I did contact Paul Zalon directly, he, like Susan and me, would become a target of the FBI for what he knew about incidents and circumstances surrounding wife Susan Ei's suspicious death. Always as I pursued answers to her death as best I could, I tried to be mindful and careful about putting anyone else at risk, of getting anyone else killed or driven into a state of extreme fear and sense of helplessness.

Once in a while I took a photograph of the license plate of a car parked near the house, or made it look like I did. I deleted what photos I did take soon after I took them. There was no reason to keep them as I knew that no law-enforcement people were going to investigate my complaint of witness intimidation, and even if anyone did investigate to find out who the car was registered to or even who may have been inside it, they would claim that there was no law against parking on the street where they had. My purpose in taking a photograph of a license plate or seeming to was to show the FBI that I recognized that they were surveilling me too in my walks past Susan's house.

There was a few times when the FBI presence and involvement in my looks at Susan's house were different or more elaborate than cars parked on the road near it. One time there was one of those electricity utility trucks with a hoist with a bucket that can be raised so a workman can work on lines or connections at poles parked not far from Susan's house on the same side of the road. The hoist was up, with a man fiddling with lines connected to a pole. One of the FBI's preferred surveillance techniques is posing as workmen such as utility company workers that are familiar to residents of neighborhoods. Parked not far from the utility company truck that was near Susan's house was a Fairfield police car. The FBI likes to often involve others in its ruses so a to make them appear to actually be workmen attending to some task; although to ones like me who know they are being targeted, such ruses are usually seen for what they are. As or the Fairfield police car in the sham near Susan's house, Fairfield police have been malfeasant with respect to FBI crimes and corruption at the Pequot Library and elsewhere in Fairfield.

Other times there were smaller utility trucks parked along Pequot Avenue within sight of Susan's house, and thus my sight when I walked by it. Once there were two SUVs parked on the road in front of the house to the west of Susan's, at the top of the same hill Susan's was on. There were a younger man and woman — both 30 or so — in the yard of the house as if inspecting it as realtors or prospective buyers. The back doors of their SUVs were opened upward so that the license plates couldn't be seen, or photographed without me holding my iPhone up over the upwardly-opened back doors. I wasn't interested in doing this though. I didn't take photographs of every vehicle parked by Susan's house. I did this less and less the more time I walked by the house, having verified for myself that the cars were part of the FBI surveillance of me when they stopped showing up or when they did, would pull away as I approached them and so could not get a photograph of the license plate.

There were a few times I saw something at Susan's house that indicated that I was not the only one being surveilled with what the respective individual would get out of this. When the FBI is being mostly apparent in its surveillance activities, this is to intimidate the individual being surveilled. For instance, if the FBI thought that I was involved in criminal activity, it would have me under surveillance for the purpose of gaining evidence or trapping me in some criminal act. The same for Paul Zalon whom I came to realize was also under surveillance, as the FBI wanted me to realize by incidents it made apparent to me in some of my walks by the house.

The first of these after about four or five walks was a younger Black man about in his late 20s walking in the cobblestone parking area. As I passed along the front of the house heading to the Fairfield railroad station, as always, I looked into the open cobblestoned area expecting to see the husband's blue BMW parked where in ordinarily was. As I looked left this time, there was a medium-built on the thin side, about six-foot or a couple of inches taller, Black man who walked across the front of the husband's parked BMW toward another smaller car, though not a sports car or compact. I was so surprised to see him that I looked quickly, and made no attempt to take in details of his features. Not only was my reaction one of surprise, but the thoughts that sprung into my mind from my experiences in being targeted for roughly ten years including the assortment of individuals the FBI employed in its intimidation, harassment, and threatening actions were jumbled. It seemed the host of individuals the FBI had involved in its surveillance activities were milling about in my mind. Besides, I did not want to appear to be threatening to the unknown man only about ten feet from me by having him think I was presuming he was maybe a trespasser opportunistically looking for something to steal or there was anything about him or the encounter alarming me so I would report it to the police.

I wasn't concerned about taking in details of the younger Black man's features because I knew even if I could describe him with some detail and did report that what to me looked like a stranger was in the house's cobblestone parking area, the situation and the man if ever found and questioned would have an explanation with Paul Zalon backing him up. But I knew different, as the FBI knew I would know. The FBI would know I had gotten part of the message, the most important part, the incident was meant to communicate. This incident was meant to communicate not only that I was continuing to be surveilled, but also add to this that Susan Ei's surviving husband was being surveilled as well. The surveillance of Paul Zalon meant more than he was being watched like me — Paul Zalon was being controlled, like his deceased wife Susan. Paul Zalon was being intimidated, intimidated not to divulge anything about the death of his wife who had been put to stalking me as part of the FBI's intimidation of me, not to divulge anything to me, but also not to divulge anything to anyone. Knowing the FBI's involvement with his wife, and that she was now dead, Paul Zalon was particularly vulnerable. The FBI's intimidation of him was particularly credible.

There were other incidents going beyond vehicles parking near the house which similarly involved different individuals that I would connect with Paul Zalon and his situation following the death of Susan. Although there were individuals in the parked vehicles as I could see, they remained in them. Individuals moving about however were something different. With them, seeing their actions, it was almost like I was interacting with them; which I was in a way in that the FBI was using them to send the message to me that Paul Zalon was under their control. It was like I was watching aspects of a drama unfold before my eyes with a concomitant shift in my awareness.

After the first sight of the younger Black man in the cobblestone area of Susan's house, now Paul Zalon's property, the next incident of a individual wanting me to realize Paul Zalon was under FBI surveillance and influence was a man about 40 standing on the steps to the front door of the house past Susan's to the west, toward Southport center, on the same stretch of hill as Susan's. This day, coming from the opposite direction to the post office rather than away from it having taken a bus to check mail rather than the train as I usually did, and gotten off at a stop by Pequot Avenue which would lead me to the post office, as I passed by Susan's house to my right, I caught the man in the corner of my eye. With the rise of the hill and the house being set back to be at the top of the hill, he was about fifteen yards away. I didn't give him any notice, thinking he was probably a workman or landscaper, maybe a real-estate agent looking over the house and yard.

I kept walking, looking ahead, staying alert for passing traffic since there was no sidewalk along this part of Pequot Avenue. As I moved along so that the man was off behind my right shoulder, before I moved farther away to the frontage of the adjacent property, the man shouted out a "hello" to me. I lifted my right arm a bit as if to wave, acknowledging I had heard him. I wasn't interested in engaging with him in anyway, another FBI agent. In this incident of not acknowledging the man by at least looking at him so that he was sure I had seen him, the FBI agent didn't want to risk the loss of another staged incident to impress on me that it was keeping Paul Zalon under its rein. The house next door to Susan's was close enough so that I could not mistake the repeat of the message than Paul Zalon was encircled by FBI watchers, in this incident with the suggestion that such encirclement was important enough to the FBI in keeping the true circumstances of Susan's death covered up by bringing property right next to Susan's house into their staged incidents.

The next incident was a somewhat stocky man on the front porch of the house, the only time I had ever seen anyone on the front porch. This time too I was coming from the bus stop. Of the two ways I could take to go past the house to the post office, on this day I took the one that gave me a better perspective of the house by being on the other side of the road rather than closer to the house on the walking path going with the road. I could still see all parts of the house visible from the roadway clearly, but take in more of this at once. As I approached the house and looked across the roadway at it, the man caught my eye by his movement. He was facing away from me, bent over, and looked like he was doing something at a table or piece of furniture at one end of the porch going the length of the front of the house. He was bobbing up and down slightly, and I could see his arms moving as if he was handling something. The fifteen seconds or so I watched him as I kept walking, he kept making the same movements, and he had his back to me the whole time. The scene quickly became a part of the chronology and cast of actors of my walks past Susan's house, my attention quickly, reflexively turning to the roadway and watching for traffic as I moved along.

The next incident was an encounter with another Black man by the cobblestone area in the earlier part of the fall 2023. Susan's house to my right after getting to it from the bus stop, as always I looked to the open cobblestone area taking in the house to the left beyond it as well. To my surprise in this encounter, as I looked rightward at a forty-five degree angle over the cobblestone area and toward the house, out from behind the corner of it came a younger Black man, fuller and heavier than the one I had seen in one previous encounter. I had never paid much attention to this part of the property because it was blocked off by the house and from what I could see of it, it was mostly more foliage, perhaps another one of Susan's gardens. Mildly surprised, my head stiffened as I became more alert. I wasn't fearful or guarded, but curious, looking somewhat intently to see if there were any details of this scene possibly portending something new or changed the FBI was signaling to me.

There wasn't anything new I could see except this individual, the younger, well-built Black man, coming out from behind the house into view. The scene unfolded naturally, smoothly. As the Black man saw me peering at him as if seeming to try to take a mental photograph of him, though only from my being surprised and then curious, he turned to his left, and walked away from me along a path at the left side of the shed-like building at the far end of the cobblestone area. My curiosity was quickly satisfied. Really nothing for me to see, nothing really beyond the seemingly normal, brief encounters happening regularly as I passed by Susan's house which I knew from their similarity to countless other encounters I had at grocery stores, at the post office, at libraries, in courthouses, walking along the sidewalk in Black Rock while I was doing errands, were staged FBI encounters to let me know I was constantly under surveillance.

My suspicion of FBI involvement in and degree of responsibility for the death of Susan Ei was not strengthened by the encounters at Susan's house — I was a close to certain as I could be. Nor did the encounters add to my awareness that the FBI was engaged in repressing information and knowledge about Susan's death and reports of experiences individuals, mainly Pequot Library employees, had with Susan or had heard about in the weeks leading up to her death or before that, when she had been put to stalking me which was an extension in time and expansion of locations in the targeting of me at the Pequot Library. The encounters at Susan's house did, however, heighten my alarm as to the threat to democratic civil society posed by the FBI by overt acts and effects such as I witnessed regularly and by insidious, undermining activities such as invasions of privacy, agent's interference in business activities for their own profit, and pressuring judges and lawyers I was aware of that the public is not generally aware of.

That the FBI would be involved with Susan Ei in such a way as to be involved in her untimely death and then become involved with the husband in such a way as to be present at or by Susan Ei's house when I walked by where the husband continued to live after her death when I walked by with the obvious inference that the husband knew he was being watched over at all times is to me extreme, unconscionable depravity. My suspicions are that Susan's death probably had to do with drugs; hence the hasty cremation which would destroy evidence of this. Whether this was suicide or accidental from taking too many drugs to try to deal with the extreme emotional and psychological state she was coerced into by her relationship with the FBI and her stalking of me that became exposed in the course of my lawsuit cannot be known. Openness by ones who had interaction with Susan during her last weeks, especially the husband and the daughters, would clear up questions raised by the facts that are known and related questions growing out of these. But no one is talking as the heavy, ominous hand of the FBI lays over this affair.

16. Susan Ei Day at the Pequot Library

Pequot Library children's librarian and dying suddenly when she still held this position and at the relatively young age of her early 60s, having previously been employed at area schools, and being a role model especially for girls with her education, continual self-improvement, and contributions to the library and her community, Susan Ei's death got covered in all the Fairfield county news and online media. When the cause of her death was mentioned at all, and it was in only two or three articles I read, this was attributed to breast cancer. One article wrote that she "had lost her battle with breast cancer." But as seen in her death certificate, breast cancer was not listed as the primary cause of death.

An April 5, 2017, article in the Fairfield online news publication called "Patch" was one of the first articles under he headline "Beloved Children's Librarian Dies at 64 in Fairfield":

> SOUTHPORT, CT — The Pequot Library community is mourning the loss of beloved Children's Librarian Susan Ei, who passed away March 30 at the age of 64. Known as "Miss Susan" to thousands of children and families, Ei launched Pequot's "Read to Our Bunny" program, in which library visitors can experience what she referred to as "labor-free pet ownership.
>
> The loss of Miss Susan will be felt in our hearts for a long, long time," Pequot Library Director Stephanie J. Coakley said in a statement. "Susan was deeply committed to everything Pequot Library, especially its young readers and we will greatly miss her incredible spirit for life, selfless and generous character, stylish flair, and unique talents and wisdom when it came to inspiring children to love reading and learning."
>
> Ei joined the Pequot Library in March 2003 and was promoted to full-time Children's Librarian in 2005. Ei loved education and learning and held a master's degree in Linguistics and a bachelor of arts with distinction in Art History from the University of Michigan, Ann Arbor.
>
> Before joining Pequot Library, she devoted her career to teaching English as a Second Language in a variety of settings, including but not limited to

La Guardia Community College, Housatonic Community College, Columbia University, and Greens Farms Academy in Westport.

At Pequot Library she excelled at creating exciting and unique events that centered on celebrating community and togetherness with yearly traditions including the Easter Egg Roll, Annual Potluck Supper and Campout, the 4th of July Bike Parade & Lawn Games, and Kids' Candy-making Workshop, with each event drawing an average of 250 patrons and many times nearly 500 visitors to Pequot Library.

Last year Ei welcomed 6,594 children to her children's and family programs including weekly Storytimes for newborns to 5-year-olds: Babes on a Blanket, Wiggle Ones, Wee People, and Three to Five Beehive. With a strong commitment to Pequot Library's mission to bring culture to life, Ms. Ei incorporated a variety of arts, humanities and science disciplines into all of her literary programs including nature and animals and developed signature events such as Make Dog Biscuits for Homeless Animals, Fly-Fishing on the Great Lawn, Atka the Wolf which included a wolf demonstration which taught children about animal wildlife, and Kids Knit.

Ei had a special talent to inspire children to want to explore the natural world around them through engaging programs about science experiments and even workshops about bee-keeping. Most of all she ignited a passion for reading in children of all ages with interactive Summer Reading programs and personalized book recommendations.

Ei's most unique program started in 2006 when she invented Pequot's "Read to Our Bunny" program. Thanks to Ei's innovativeness, children and adults can still experience what Ei referred to as "labor-free pet ownership;" the library's bunny lives at Pequot Library, and parents can make appointments for their child/children to read to and pet the bunny. Emerging readers have always enjoyed the fact that a rabbit does not judge if they make a mistake.

Scores of children each year "check out" the resident bunny for a stroll around the neighborhood and many plant the herb garden on the Library's grounds to help feed the bunny. Ei and her reading ambassador rabbit assistants, Blossom, Belle, and Puff touched the lives of countless children and their parents with this special reading program. Ei and her three reading ambassadors helped young readers build confidence with their

budding literacy skills and engaged even the littlest library visitors as they
played with the bunny when they stopped in Pequot Library.

Ei was generous, intelligent, free-spirited, caring, and adventurous. She
was a cowgirl at heart, and she will be dearly missed by her Pequot Library
family and friends.

Susan's April 4, 2017, obituary in the Connecticut Post newspaper relates
biographical details about her personal life and employee at the Pequot
Library while also relating traits for which she was admired and missed."

On April 4, 2017, the newspaper "Connecticut Post" published an obituary:

Susan Ei Obituary — Susan Michelle Ei

Susan Ei, born in Detroit on April 3, 1952, was a multi-faceted woman who
embraced all of humanity, animals, and the green earth with grace, gratitude,
and an unbridled spirit; she was a true original. She transitioned during a
raging rainstorm as if the universe were greeting her with wild abandon. She
lived with a deep sense of adventure, fearlessness, and excitement.

Susan was the beloved mother of Lily Ei Zalon and Annie June Zalon. She was
the deeply loved wife of Paul Zalon, sister of David Ei, Carol DeJong, Ellen
Masta and Philip Willson.

Susan had an MA from the University of Michigan and was the Children's
Librarian at the Pequot Library for the past 14 years. She and her assistant,
Belle the Bunny, touched the lives of countless children and their parents. She
knew how to play.

Susan was authentically wise and spoke from a place of love, acceptance, and
joy. She expressed her opinions through actions rather than lengthy debates.

She had an enormous impact on all who knew her, near and far. Her beautiful
soul emanated through her constant smile, her infectious laugh, and her
willingness to live life with gusto. Her collection of friends spans her entire
life, multiple locations, all walks of life, young and old.

She created unique and welcoming spaces everywhere she went: at home, at work, while entertaining scores of family and friends. Like a painter and sculptor; she could weave a one of a kind tableaux in an empty room.

Her legacy to her daughters, Lily and Annie, was planting the seeds in them to move in the world with strength, confidence, imagination, intelligence, storytelling, appreciation for beauty and nature, authenticity, and a deep well of caring and loving.

The local online news publication "Daily Voice" reported toward the end of its notice, "Services will be held at The Unitarian Church of Westport at 10 Lyons Plains Road, Westport, on Thursday, April 6, at 1 p.m. All are welcome...The Pequot Library will be closed Thursday in honor of [Susan Ei's] longstanding commitment and dedication to the library and to allow her colleagues and patrons to attend her memorial service." By then, of course, Susan had been cremated even though in her will she left funds specifically for a funeral service. I got a copy of her will through the probate process required for my lawsuit to continue after her death by bringing in her estate and its executor, who was husband Paul Zalon.

Considering Susan's long-time association with Pequot Library and her prominence and effectiveness as children's librarian, the library wished to commemorate her further, to keep her memory alive mainly by holding activities she was associated with particularly. Primary among these was an annual activity called "Miss Susan's Summer Supper and Cookout." A typical annual notice of this event in the Fairfield Patch with online distribution throughout Fairfield county was, "June 9, 2023, Miss Susan's Summer Supper and Cookout, Fri, Jun 9, 2023, at 6:30 PM. Join in a favorite traditional community event — a tribute to Children's Librarian, Susan Ei, on Pequot Library's one-of-a-kind Great Lawn! Enjoy hamburgers, hot dogs, and veggie burgers, or BYO Picnic. The Merwin Mountain Band will play live music. Take part in lawn games including badminton, ping pong, and spinnaker. Roast s'mores around the campfire. As the sun sets enjoy taking a closer look at the night sky through our telescope...Sign up for your Summer Programs Attendee Card and start earning stamps by participating in our summer events and activities. Come for any part of the evening, or pitch your tent and camp all night...Remember to bring a pillow for the Big Pillow Fight!Schedule of events: 6:30 PM: BYO Picnic Supper; 7:15 PM:

Outdoor Concert with the Merwin Mountain Band; 9:00 PM: The Big Pillow Fight For All Ages, Pet Friendly."

The were also memorials for Susan in the library annual reports. Couples or individuals had made donations to the library noting that they were made in memory of Susan Ei, and would be recognized as such by citing of the donor's names below a heading "In Memory of Susan Ei". I sent in a donation of $50 to be recognized in memory of Susan in 2022 shortly after my prosecution for trespass at the library was dismissed by the state's attorney handling the case and the judge at the hearing. I was arrested in 2019 after going to the library knowing I would be arrested since I saw this as the best way, the most direct way, and probably the only way to expose the crimes and corruption I knew was going on among library employees and FBI agents and accomplices connected to them.

The trespass case against me was dismissed in May 2022 as trial was imminent, as I expected it would be since my court-appointed public defender stand-by counsel, the prosecutor, and the judge learned that I was going to expose the crimes and corruption in my testimony on behalf of my defense of myself at a trial. While it lasted, the prosecution was productive for me as a self-represented defendant — someone who represents himself in a case rather than being represented by a lawyer— since in the course of it, I obtained documents containing false or misleading statements by certain library employees, saw attempts in other documents by police officers to cover up or distract from my accusations against employees working with FBI agents for hostile acts against me at the library, and observed as a series of prosecutors and judges too became convinced of my innocence as I related facts about my case and divulged aspects of my defense in court hearings for the close to three years the case was prosecuted. I could have ended it earlier myself by accepting deals offered by prosecutors, but I was finding that learning about court procedures and the maneuverings of prosecutors and judges and how they handled information from police officers would be useful in my litigation against the Pequot Library and individuals at the to come. In my defense of myself in the trespass case, I was in effect building a stronger malicious prosecution case against the library and certain employees and also their relationship with FBI and Fairfield police officers.

In making my $50 donation designating it was being made in commemoration of Susan Ei, my name would be printed in the "Memorials"

Ordinarily, the name of the person making a donation in memory of someone deceased would be printed under a heading of the person's name in the section of the forthcoming Pequot Library annual report titled "Memorials." In my case, I expected my name would appear under the heading "In Memory of Susan Ei," like the names of other individuals who had donated in Susan's memory in previous years had appeared in respective annual reports. But this was not to be. In less than a week after I made the donation, I received a letter from the lawyer who had represented Pequot Library defendants in lawsuits I had pursued and who had appeared at court hearings during my trespass case at the Bridgeport courthouse G. A. 2 on behalf of the Pequot Library employees, whom he called "victims", that my $50 donation was being returned to me.

When making a memorial donation, the donor can name someone who the library will notify about the donation. I named Paul Zalon. I don't know if he ever was notified about the donation I tried to make in memory of his deceased wife. In remembrance of Susan, the library started what was called Miss Susan's Summer Supper and Cookout, held on an evening in June when the weather is usually warm enough in Connecticut to be outside. This annual event ran for a few years since Susan's death in 2017. Online information records that it was held in 2023; but information for 2024 says that it was canceled.